FOUNTAINS ABBEY

THE CISTERCIANS IN NORTHERN ENGLAND

Glyn Coppack

TEMPUS

First published 2004
Reprinted 2006

Tempus Publishing Ltd
The Mill, Brimscombe Port
Stroud, Gloucestershire GL5 2QG
www.tempus-publishing.com

British Library Cataloguing in Publication Data.
A catalogue record for this book is available from the British Library.

ISBN 0 7524 2546 3

Typesetting and origination by Tempus Publishing.
Printed and bound in Great Britain.

FOUNTAINS ABBEY

THE CISTERCIANS IN NORTHERN ENGLAND

CONTENTS

PREFACE

In multi-cultural and multi-faith twenty-first-century Britain, the medieval monastic church continues to fascinate many people for a great many reasons, some of them to do with the original concept but most to do with modern values. There are some 200 monastic ruins in England, many in attractive countryside and accessible to visitors, and without a doubt the finest of these is Fountains Abbey. A roofless ruin since 1540 and set in the managed late-eighteenth-century landscape of Studley Royal, it has been popular with tourists since the middle years of the nineteenth century. Privately owned until 1966, it is now a National Trust property, although the ruins of the abbey are maintained by English Heritage. Fountains Abbey and Studley Royal was inscribed as a World Heritage Site by UNESCO in 1986, a signifier of its international importance. Some 300,000 visitors a year also indicate how it is perceived. All of this is the very opposite of what the founding monastic community intended.

When a small band of monks came to Skelldale in the mid-winter of 1132 they had little notion of what they were starting. Theirs was a frontier settlement, a mission-centre for the young Cistercian order, set 'far from the concourse of men' where monks could follow the rule of St Benedict in communion with nature far from the distractions of the world outside. They settled in the wood of Herleshowe, for as their mentor Bernard of Clairvaux taught 'you will find in woods something you will never find in books – stones and trees will teach you a lesson you never heard from masters in the schools'. It was to be a hard lesson but a profitable one. The rags-to-riches story of Fountains Abbey paralleled the meteoric success of the Cistercian order itself, and Fountains provides one of the finest examples of the rise and decline of the order in Europe, where success sapped the spirituality that drove it. Within 50 years of its foundation, powered by religious fervour and funded by the income of a substantial and well-managed estate, Fountains was the principal house of the order in England, the mother house of eight successful colonies and rivalled the first daughter-houses of Cîteaux itself.

The story of Fountains Abbey is written not only in contemporary documents but also in the surviving fabric of its buildings and its buried archaeology. This story has been unravelled over the past 30 years in the course of the abbey's conservation by English Heritage and its predecessor, the Department of the Environment. My own involvement with Fountains began in 1977 and has lasted for 25 years, during which time there has been a complete reappraisal of the monastery's development, making Fountains without doubt the best understood Cistercian monastery in Europe. Our knowledge is still imperfect and the full story can never be known for the site is an incomplete shell that is only documented for part of its history, and its archaeology has only been sampled. Conservation and study will continue for another 20 years, and it is certain that much more information will come to light. In particular, the greater part of the earliest monastic buildings, of both timber and stone, remain unexcavated, a wonderful resource for future generations whose techniques of excavation and information retrieval will be much more sophisticated than our own. Since the first publication of this book in 1993 there have been a number of significant developments: geophysical survey has revealed the mass of buildings that occupied the empty area in front of the standing west range; the large scale excavation of Sawley Abbey, a grand-daughter house of Fountains with the largest known collection of early timber buildings has been published; and Peter Fergusson and Stuart Harrison have published their monograph on Rievaulx Abbey, Fountains' great rival in Yorkshire. As a result, it is now possible to better understand the context of the buildings at Fountains. Fountains remains the most intensively studied Cistercian house in Europe.

The site has been the subject of antiquarian study since the seventeenth century and archaeological research since the late eighteenth. Its study by Richard Walbran, Gordon Hill, Arthur Reeve, and William St John Hope in the nineteenth century placed Fountains in the forefront of monastic studies where it remains today. In the twentieth century, that study was continued by John Bilson, the Rev. A.W. Oxford, W.T. Lancaster, Roy Gilyard-Beer, B. Waites, R.A. Donkin and David Michelmore. By the late 1970s it could reasonably be assumed that there was little more to learn about the site, its history, and its economy. At the time I would have believed this myself, but events have since proved I could not have been more wrong.

I owe my involvement with Fountains to John Weaver who invited me to undertake excavations in advance of the Department of the Environment conservation programme from 1977, the first major campaign of excavation since the late 1880s. The success of that work was greatly enhanced by the generosity of the late Roy Gilyard-Beer (G-B) who shared his own unrivalled knowledge of the site and many others with me and who was always willing to debate matters of interpretation. He had discovered the earlier stone church in 1968 but had been unsure of its interpretation. When it was re-excavated in 1979-80 it was Gilyard-Beer who persuaded me to extend my research to the early cloister buildings rather than to continue the work I was planning in Lincolnshire (which is still waiting to be done).

From 1984-1989 I was additionally fortunate to be the Inspector of Ancient Monuments responsible for Fountains, during which time a detailed survey of the site was undertaken, first by Judith Roebuck and latterly by Keith Emerick and Kate Wilson. They have all willingly shared their knowledge of the site with me and provided a sounding board against which I have tested many of my own ideas. They have allowed me to include their work here in advance of their own publication, for which I am particularly grateful. English Heritage has no copyright on research at Fountains and the monument continues to be the subject of international study. I have drawn widely on the work of others as they have drawn on my work. In particular, two scholars deserve my particular thanks: Stuart Harrison who has made an extensive study of the loose architectural detail from the site, partly for English Heritage and partly for his own private research, and made available his own unpublished drawings; and Peter Fergusson, now a good friend, who taught me to see Fountains in the wider context of the Cistercian order. Both have helped me to understand the monument in ways that do not come easily to an archaeologist and have also corrected my worst errors of fact and interpretation. They bear no responsibility for those that remain. Others have helped in different ways: Dr Christopher Young ensured that the programme of archaeological research that lies behind this book was funded adequately and was allowed to continue; my successors the late Jim Lang and Keith Emerick who have continued the work I began; and the National Trust and English Heritage teams caring for Fountains who appreciate the importance of a proper study of the monument as it is conserved for posterity. My debt to scholarship is no less great. I have benefited from the advice of many scholars, among them the late Professor Maurice Barley, Dr Philip Dixon, Dr Peter Addyman, Dr Christopher Norton, Dr Jennie Stopford, Dr Stuart Wrathmell, Dr David Robinson, Dr Susan Wright, Professor David Walsh, Dr Terryl Kinder, Steve Moorhouse, and Richard Halsey. I have freely quarried from the works of others and this is acknowledged in the text; the interpretation of their work, however, is my own.

Peter Kemmis Betty, who originally published this book in the B.T. Batsford/English Heritage series, was kind enough to commission an updated and corrected version even though he had suffered the pain of getting the original one out of me. Otherwise it would have quietly disappeared into the second-hand market. As with the original version, much of the artwork was produced by Karen Guffog, Kate Morton, and Judith Dobie at English Heritage and by Simon Hayfield who worked at Fountains with me over 20 years ago. Photographs come from my own collection and the English Heritage Photographic Library or are acknowledged in the captions. The National Trust kindly provided the cover illustration and copies of the Nebot paintings.

Working at or on Fountains Abbey has always been a joy and a privilege – it is a site that never fails to surprise, and it is rare that I visit and do not discover something new. It is a testament to those who built it, lived and died there, and to those responsible for its continuing care. This book is my contribution to its continuing story.

Glyn Coppack
Goxhill
October 2002

1

THE NEW SOLDIERS OF CHRIST

On 27 December 1132, Archbishop Thurstan of York brought a group of 13 monks from York to the valley of the River Skell 6km to the west of Ripon in a place called the wood of Herleshowe. Here he gave them land to establish a monastery, a wild and inhospitable place, more fitting to be the lair of wild beasts than of men as the abbey's later chronicle recorded. Initially the monks sheltered under the rocks of the valley and then under a great elm tree. From this unpromising beginning grew the great Cistercian abbey of Fountains (**colour plates 1** & **2**). How this came about, and how Fountains came to be one of the greatest abbeys of its order and one of the most important monastic sites in Europe, is truly remarkable. Contemporary documents, surviving buildings, and the evidence of archaeology together make Fountains Abbey the most informative of any Cistercian abbey in Europe, and show clearly the development of the most remarkable reform movement in Christendom.

The ruins of Fountains Abbey comprise one of the finest and most extensive monastic sites in Europe and reflect the wealth and ambitions of the Cistercian monks who lived there for just over four centuries. What can be seen today is no more than the skeleton of an abbey. All of the furnishings and fittings, most of the wall painting and the silence of monastic life have gone, to be replaced by eighteenth century landscaping and twentieth century conservation for the heritage market. Enough remains, however, to enable the recreation of much that has been lost to spoliation and weathering and to reconstruct the story of Fountains' development. Although it was to become the greatest Cistercian abbey in Britain, its present appearance belies its early history, for the first years of the monastery's existence were fraught with poverty and uncertainty. The ruins that survive are, in fact, the remains of the third abbey to be built on the site; each phase represents a stage in the development of the Cistercian order internationally.

The origins of the Cistercian order

It is not in Skelldale that the story begins, for the origins of Fountains Abbey can be traced back to a strangely similar occurrence in France. The tenth and eleventh centuries were a time of reform in the monastic world, as Benedictine monks attempted to return to an earlier simplicity in both their lives and their liturgies.

In 910 the foundation of a new abbey at Cluny near Mâcon in Burgundy had marked a revival in monastic life. Originally a house of Benedictine monks, Cluny benefited from a series of very able abbots who insisted on a stricter observance of the early sixth-century rule of St Benedict, making Cluny the centre of an influential monastic revival not only in France but throughout Europe. What began at Cluny was to continue as other groups of monks sought a more exacting way to reach God through prayer and manual work.

In 1098, a group of dissenting monks left the Cluniac abbey of Molesme in southern Burgundy, frustrated in an attempt to bring their lives into an even stricter accordance with the precepts of St Benedict that were central to monastic life in medieval Europe. Led by their prior, Robert, who had earlier experimented with hermit life at Sèche Fontaine in the forests of Burgundy, 21 monks left Molesme to build a new monastery where they could enjoy a harsh but simple life. They called their new house, built on swampy land 22.5km south of Dijon, the New Minster (*monasterium novum*). In Latin, the common monastic language, the site was called *Cistercium* from *cisterna*, a marsh. In modern French it is called Cîteaux.

Benedictine monasticism was almost 700 years old when Cîteaux was founded and had grown away from the way of life its founder had intended. By the early years of the ninth century, the medieval concept of the monastery was fully developed, with a great church and cloister ranges providing the enclosure for the religious at the centre of a supporting array of courts and service buildings. Monasteries were wealthy institutions supported by vast agricultural estates and their wealth went into the creation of fine buildings and developing liturgies. The St Gall plan, the schematic design for a new Benedictine monastery in Switzerland, drawn up in about 820, shows the scale and complexity which had become the norm for an important monastery. At the centre was the cloister, with its garden, the very heart of monastic life, with the common dormitory on its east side, the refectory on its south side, and a store house on the west. The fourth side of the cloister was closed by the great church, the largest of all the buildings of the monastery. Surrounding these core buildings was a whole series of smaller but no less important structures: kitchens, brew houses, bake houses, smithy, cooper's shop, animal houses, infirmary, gardens, and cemetery. Not only monks lived in the monastery but also their servants and workmen, and the whole was divided into three strictly controlled parts: the 'house' restricted to the religious themselves; the inner court which was a semi-public area providing for guests; and the outer court which was the service area where animals were kept, grain stored, and industry practised. While the cloister buildings were quiet and provided seclusion, the inner and outer courts were rather noisier, distracting and the latter area was occasionally unpleasant. The aim was to make the monastery efficient, self-supporting and self-perpetuating, supported by a network of agricultural estates.

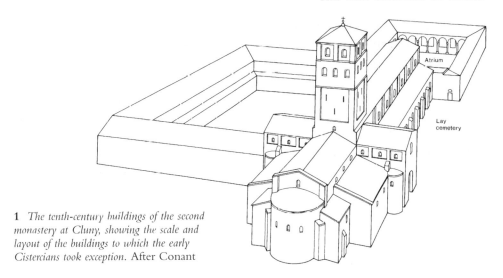

Atrium

Lay cemetery

1 *The tenth-century buildings of the second monastery at Cluny, showing the scale and layout of the buildings to which the early Cistercians took exception.* After Conant

Efficiency brought wealth, and the only outlet for surplus money was the acquisition of more land or building. At Cluny (**1**) this had resulted in the construction of a monumental church in the second half of the tenth century, the centre of a highly developed ritual. The dissenting monks from Molesme wanted none of this, but sought to return to first principles, redefining monasticism and building crude timber buildings with their own hands. In 1099, Robert and half of his followers were forced to return to Molesme, but in spite of this serious set-back the new community of *Cistercium* survived and began the building of a simple stone church and cloister which was sufficiently complete to be consecrated in 1106. Stone buildings imply both the support of patrons and permanence of the community, though there is no suggestion that at this point the monks saw themselves as anything other that simple Benedictines, living in accordance with a stricter interpretation of the rule of St Benedict than their brothers at Molesme.

Central to the early years of life at *Cistercium* was Harding, an Englishman who had been a monk of the cathedral priory of Sherborne in Dorset, left the cloister to go on pilgrimage to Rome, where he took the name of Stephen, and who had joined the community at Molesme in 1085. He had risen there to the rank of sub-prior and was one of the most insistent agitators for reform. According to a fellow west-countryman, William of Malmesbury, writing his *Gesta Regum Anglorum* in 1122-3, it was Harding who was initially responsible for the dissent at Molesme. In 1109 he was elected abbot of *Cistercium* (**colour plate 3**), a post he was to hold until his death in 1135. His strict interpretation of the Benedictine rule, and particularly its insistence on poverty and manual labour, almost destroyed the community, for disease and death seriously reduced numbers.

The new monastery's reputation for discipline and simple living was, however, its salvation, attracting many recruits of exceptional ability, to the extent that a second monastery had to be established at La Ferté in 1113. Another colony was established at Pontigny in 1114, and two more at Morimond and Clairvaux in 1115. With Cîteaux, these four colonies were to form the core of the most successful monastic reform movement of the Middle Ages (2). By 1119 there were five more monasteries established and the time had come formally to create a new Order; this was to be known from Cîteaux as the Cistercian Order.

The creation of a rule

The rapid growth of Cîteaux and its four daughter houses required the development of a monastic philosophy, and it was Stephen Harding who was responsible for the early codification of the community's ideals – spiritual, social and architectural. His approach was fundamental, taking the rule that St Benedict had written for his monastery of Monte Casino in the early years of the sixth century, but also going back to the earlier teachings of Sts Basil and John Cassian. Central to life at Cîteaux and her colonies were two documents: the *Exordium Parvum* (A Little Introduction), an account of the foundation of Cîteaux, and the *Carta Caritatis* (The Charter of Love), an outline of the Cistercians' constitution, both largely the work of Harding and dating to around 1119 though they contain earlier material. They set an uncompromising insistence on poverty, simplicity of life, and the need physically to separate the communities from the outside world and its distractions. The dependence on the outside world for financial support, that is the income from manors and churches given by patrons to support religious communities, was seen as the cause of worldliness in other orders that distracted monks from their true purpose, to serve God by prayer and manual work.

To prevent disturbance, the Cistercians placed their monasteries away from other settlements 'far from the concourse of men' and sought to be self-sufficient, renouncing all cash revenues and feudal ties. Their economy, without which they could not survive, was to be land-based. To achieve such an economy without being reliant on feudal labour, the Cistercians developed the concept of lay brothers or *conversi* who would work their estates while bound by monastic discipline. Older orders had used small numbers of lay brethren but it was the Cistercians who first recruited them in large numbers to service their abbeys. They were effectively second-class monks, and offered on a large scale a chance previously denied to the uneducated labouring and servant classes to enter monastic life. The rapid growth of the order and its capacity to support itself was very much due to this concept. While the presence of lay brothers enabled the order to develop a highly centralised method of farming (see Chapter Five), the need to accommodate two separate communities within a single monastery required a fundamental re-arrangement of the traditional monastic plan.

St Benedict required his monks to divide their lives into three parts: the saying of the church offices (*opus Dei*); spiritual reading and meditation (*lectio*

2 *The location of Cîteaux, her first daughter houses, and other sites mentioned in the text*

divina); and manual labour (*opus manuum*). By the end of the eleventh century this three-way division had virtually disappeared. Ulrich, writing of life at Cluny itself around 1090, tells us that so much time was taken up by the church offices which had become highly developed rituals that the monks had no time for manual labour and hardly any time for reading. The Cistercians ruthlessly redefined the monastic timetable. Beginning with the *opus Dei* they cut all additions with the exception of the morning Mass to the outline provided by St Benedict. Ceremonial was reduced and musical chant simplified. With time spent in church reduced, both reading and manual work could be restored. Importantly, an opportunity was provided for private prayer.

To ensure the stability of these reforms, the *Carta Caritatis* provided the model for a central authority within the order that remained a masterpiece of planning. Each year, every abbot was to attend a general chapter at Cîteaux to enforce collective discipline and to enact statutes by which the development and direction of the order was to be controlled. Additionally, a cellular structure was created by which abbeys were arranged in 'families' headed by Cîteaux and its four original colonies. Each new monastery was the responsibility of the abbey it was founded from, and the abbot of that house was required to visit the colony or 'daughter-house' annually. Papal consent was obtained to exempt Cistercian monasteries from visitation and correction by diocesan bishops, ensuring that no outside influence could distract the movement of reform. So successful was that reform that within 40 years of the foundation of Cîteaux's first daughter-house of La Ferté there were 339 monasteries within the order, a number which had risen to 525 by the close of the twelfth century. It is difficult now to appreciate the missionary zeal of Stephen Harding's 'new soldiers of Christ', the name they were given very early in their history.

Their strict discipline and asceticism appealed strongly to the aristocracy who formed the European military class, though they did not necessarily impress other monks. Abbot Peter (the Venerable) of Cluny was appalled by what he saw, writing in 1127 that 'it is unbecoming that monks which are the fine linen of the sanctuary should be begrimed with dirt and bent down with rustic labours'. To the Benedictine William of Malmesbury, however, 'the Cistercians … are a model for all, a mirror for the diligent, a spur to the indolent'. Rejecting the black habits of the Benedictines and Cluniacs, the Cistercians wore undyed or white habits, from which they became commonly known as the 'White Monks' (**colour plates 4** & **5**). Their lay brothers had brown habits to distinguish them. Both were forbidden undershirts and breeches, an unheard of austerity in the colder climate of Northern Europe. Their diet was sparse and unremittingly vegetarian, their life was undoubtedly harsh, and to a certain extent anti-intellectual. However, it provided, in the words of St Aelred, Abbot of Rievaulx, 'everywhere peace, everywhere serenity, and a marvellous freedom from the tumult of the world'.

St Bernard of Clairvaux

The Cistercian way of life attracted men of outstanding ability to the cloister, none more remarkable than a young Burgundian nobleman, Bernard des Fontaines, who entered Cîteaux with a group of his followers in 1113. Bernard's progression from novice to abbot of the daughter-house of Clairvaux in less than three years was meteoric, and as Bernard of Clairvaux he was eventually to replace the aging Stephen Harding as the driving force of the order. The fraudulent alteration of Cistercian documents after St Bernard's death in 1153 has tended to take the credit for much of the reform from Stephen Harding, but the two men were very different and almost complementary in their reforming zeal. Harding was a monks' monk while Bernard of Clairvaux took the influence of the Cistercian reform to a wider audience. He combined the two qualities of great austerity and boundless energy, and was 'the counsellor of Popes and Kings'. It is difficult to decide today how much Bernard contributed to the development of the order, but his sermons, letters and his biography, the *Vita Prima*, edited by Geoffroi d'Auxerre tell us something about his character and achievements. All have to be studied with caution, and particularly the *Vita Prima* which, though begun in Bernard's lifetime was conceived as hagiography and not objective history. Some of it was clearly written with the benefit of hindsight!

For our purposes, the most important document is Bernard's *Apologia ad Gulielmum* (Discourse to William), which was written to the Benedictine abbot William of St Thiery in about 1124 to justify the Cistercians' attack on the sumptuous buildings (**3**) and elaborate rituals of the Cluniacs and which gives an insight into contemporary Cistercian ideology. He wrote of 'the immense height of the churches, their immoderate length, their superfluous breadth, costly polishings and strange designs that, while they attract the eye of the worshipper, hinder his attention', suggesting that the Cistercians themselves favoured the opposite. He fulminated equally about great brass candlesticks, immoderate dress and rich food. Here he seems to have gone beyond Stephen Harding's philosophy and set a standard to which his order should direct itself. Some scholars have seen in St Bernard's criticism the seeds of Cistercian architectural development which is today particularly discernible within the family of Clairvaux, for the order was to build simple and unadorned churches that reflected Bernard's puritanism.

At the time that the *Apologia* was written, however, the Cistercians had yet to begin the building of major churches, and Bernard's comments, written in his cell in the temporary wooden monastery at Clairvaux, reflect the deliberately small and austere churches that the order was just beginning to adopt in the early 1120s. It was not until a great new church was built at Clairvaux between 1135 and 1145 that a model existed for the 'Bernardine' church which has come to be accepted as the culmination of Bernard's architectural philosophy and which is clearly the model for the earliest surviving churches of the Clairvaulx family in England and Scotland. Bernard initially opposed the building of this great new church which was needed to house his rapidly growing community and only agreed to it after much soul-searching; he always remembered the first buildings at Clairvaux with great affection.

Bernard was a great organiser who saw the Cistercian reform as a missionary cause to be carefully planned and executed, building up the family of Clairvaux with a military precision in which he took the closest interest. Under his direction, Clairvaux began to outshine Cîteaux itself, and by his death in 1153 some 159 out of a total of 339 daughter-houses belonged to its filiation.

The mission to England

In 1131, Abbot Bernard of Clairvaux began the systematic colonisation of northern England and Scotland. Writing to Henry I of England Bernard claimed 'In your land there is an outpost of my Lord and your Lord, an outpost he has preferred to die for than to lose. I have proposed to occupy it and am sending men from my army who will, if it is not displeasing to you, claim it, recover it, and restore it with a strong hand'. Emissaries sent with the letter were to survey the new site and report back to Clairvaux on its suitability. Behind the letter were the actions of Walter Espec, lord of Helmsley and a Royal Justiciar, a vassal of both Henry I of England and David I of Scotland. Espec was no stranger to monastic reform. Following Henry's example he had brought Augustinian canons to Kirkham in Yorkshire in 1121-2 and he was now interested in settling the militant Cistercians on his lands with the support of his two feudal lords and the reforming Archbishop of York, Thurstan. A small colony of Yorkshire monks had entered Clairvaux and perhaps we should also see their desire to return to their homeland with the seeds of the Cistercian reform.

The Cistercians had already been settled at Waverley in Surrey in 1128 with the support of William Giffard, Bishop of Winchester, the colony coming from l'Aumône in Normandy, itself of the family of Cîteaux. Bernard appears willingly to have grasped the chance to establish the family of Clairvaux in the North, almost in competition with Waverley which was to colonise the South, Wales, and Ireland. Both houses were to take advantage of wild, inhospitable, and uncultivated land, areas ideal for Cistercian expansion.

On 5 March 1132 a colony of 12 Clairvaux monks led by their abbot, William, a scholar from York who had entered Clairvaux and served as

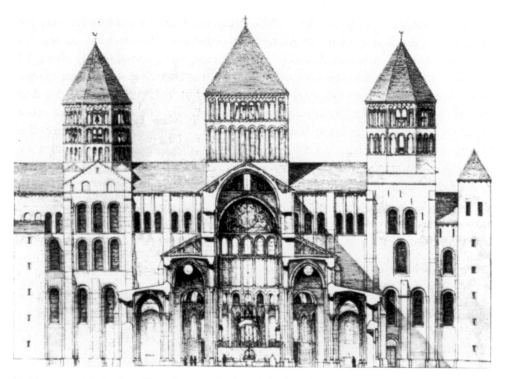

3 *The great third church at Cluny, begun at the close of the eleventh century, appalled Bernard of Clairvaux with its ostentation and distracting ornament. Only the north transept has survived, but when complete it was the greatest monastic church in Europe*

Bernard's secretary, was settled in the valley of the River Rye 3.2km (2 miles) from Espec's castle at Helmsley. The foundation of Rievaulx Abbey as it was soon to be called caused an immediate explosion of monastic fervour in the North of England. Particularly affected were the two great Benedictine establishments, the cathedral priory of Durham and York Abbey, both rich houses with a growing reputation for worldliness. Both were ripe for the Cistercian reform, but it was at York that the missionary Cistercians had their greatest effect. Their reputation of sanctity, poverty and simplicity appealed to six members of the York community, Ranulph, Thomas, Gamel, Hamo, Walter, and Gregory, who, led by the sacrist, Richard, began to press their aging abbot Geoffrey for the return of their house to sound Benedictine values.

Dissent at York Abbey

Abbot Geoffrey was not prepared to see his authority questioned or his abbey reformed. Although the dispute first came to light in April, it dragged on throughout the summer of 1132 and the original group of dissenters was joined by the prior, another Richard, the sub-prior Gervase, Geoffrey, Robert of Subella, Radulf, Alexander, and Robert, a former monk of Whitby. It was not until 28 June that Prior Richard put the case of the would-be reformers to the abbot in writing. The abbot delayed his reply until after 8 September, but the dispute had reached the ears of Archbishop Thurstan who decided, as was his right, to visit the abbey and resolve the situation on 6 October. By then, 13 members of the community were calling for reform and there seemed little hope of compromise. Abbot Geoffrey gathered support from the heads of other Benedictine and Cluniac houses and when the Archbishop arrived there was a brawl in the cloister as these black monks tried to prevent him entering the chapter-house. Thurstan had little choice but to place the abbey under an interdict, forbidding the community to celebrate divine services until they had purged their contempt, and to take the dissenting monks into his own protection in his palace at York. They were to remain there until Christmas when they accompanied Thurstan to Ripon. Two days later they were taken to Skelldale and Fountains Abbey was established. In addition to a plot of land for the abbey itself, Thurstan provided an endowment of two carucates of land at nearby Sutton to support the community. Prior Richard was elected the first abbot of the new monastery on the same day.

The earliest years of Fountains Abbey

The earliest history of Fountains is known from an eye-witness account recorded by Brother Hugh of Kirkstall around 1206. Abbot John of York, mindful of the

Cistercian tradition of recording the 'official' history of each monastery, advised Hugh to consult Serlo, then in his ninety-ninth year, who had been a member of the early Fountains community. Although he had not entered Fountains until 1137, he had been in York at the time of the dispute and was related to some of the dissidents. He remained at Fountains until March 1147 when he left as one of the group which was eventually to settle a daughter-house at Kirkstall, and up to that date he would have shared the experiences of the founding community in its formative years. Thereafter, his story is based on information received. It is less detailed and admitted to contain the memories of others. Hugh and Serlo's history, the *Narratio de fundatione Fontanis Monasterii* (the Story of the Foundation of Fountains Abbey) is a remarkably informative document, despite the fact that it shows Serlo to have been a true Cistercian, indifferent to buildings and the passing of time. The few dates given are interpolated by Hugh from other sources, for Serlo was content with 'after some days' or 'not long afterwards'. His phrases are also typical of his Cistercian indoctrination, for they are taken from the Vulgate bible (principally from the Book of Isaiah) and early Cistercian sources. How much of the similarity between Serlo's story and the early histories of Molesme, Cîteaux, and Clairvaux result from coincidence, deliberate emulation or an unconscious wish to strengthen his story, we will never know, but the parallels that emerge are truly remarkable.

The Benedictines who settled at Fountains were not provided with any shelter by the Archbishop; instead they were forced to manage as best they could in difficult circumstances. Sheltering first among the rocks and caves of the valley, they later sought the shelter of a great elm tree where they built a hut of wattles and turf. Although Thurstan had protected the monks for three months he had not provided the temporary buildings required for the settlement of any Cistercian abbey and which he must have seen when he attended the foundation ceremony at Rievaulx only nine months before. Their planting in Skelldale must have been the result of careful thought, for the site proved to be ideal, and the lack of temporary buildings should be seen in the context of the monks still being Benedictine and not subject to the Cistercian order's discipline. Indeed, they modelled their settlement on that of an earlier Benedictine abbey in Yorkshire. Benedict of Auxerre settled below an oak tree called *Strihac* on the bank of the River Ouse in 1068 to found the abbey of Selby, and it may have been the choice of the Fountains monks to seek the hardest possible beginning for their house.

The hut of wattles and turf was shortly followed by the creation of a garden for manual labour and an oratory for prayer, and it was from this rudimentary monastery that emissaries were sent to Clairvaux to seek admission into the order early in 1133. Its site in the valley is uncertain though John Leland recorded a tradition current in 1540 that the elm tree still survived, and was thus unlikely to be on the same site as the later monastic buildings, and as recently as the late eighteenth century, a rotted stump called the 'Fountains Elm' was recorded 457m east of the present abbey buildings by Christopher Husband, grandfather of the historian Richard Walbran. The stump was on the north bank of the River Skell.

The privations of the first months of settlement under the elm tree proved too great for Gervase and Radulf and they left the community to return to York, much to the disgust of their companions. In their place, however, another of the York monks, Adam, who like Robert had been a monk at Whitby, joined the Fountains community. Gervase later reappears at Fountains and it is uncertain whether he returned or that Serlo had simply confused him with another monk. Given that he was to lead the first colony from Fountains, the latter is more likely.

Abbot Bernard of Clairvaux's reply to the Fountains community can be dated by its contents, for he said he had heard of the community from his brothers William and Geoffrey. William must be the abbot of Rievaulx attending his first General Chapter at Cîteaux in September 1133, and it has been suggested that Geoffrey was Geoffroi d'Ainai, a monk of Clairvaux who might have been present at the setting out of Rievaulx in 1131-2. Bernard acceded to the convent's request and Geoffrroi d'Ainai was dispatched to Fountains, arriving late in 1133. As a monk of advanced years, skilled in Cistercian manners and particularly experienced in the instruction of communities who wished to convert to Cistercian ways, his task was to train the Fountains community in the order's philosophy and to provide them with a proper framework within which they could work and pray. Serlo tells us that under Geoffroi's instruction the Fountains monks built 'huts and offices'. This bald statement conceals the truth, for what was provided was a new timber monastery built to the model already provided at Clairvaux, and on a new site. According to the statutes of the order, this would comprise an oratory, a dormitory, a refectory, a chamber for guests and a porter's lodge, the most basic provision necessary for monastic life. No cloister was included and these buildings were intended to serve only until the community achieved stability and could afford to build permanent buildings in stone.

The timber monastery

The move to a new site effected a symbolic break with the Benedictine past, and followed a common Cistercian practice. The new site chosen at Fountains lies at the heart of the surviving ruins and excavation in 1979-80 revealed parts of two of its timber buildings below the south transept of the standing church (**4** & **5**). Though many of these buildings are described in Cistercian chronicles and later sources, for instance at Clairvaux itself (where some of them survive), at Foigny, Rievaulx and Meaux (a later daughter-house of Fountains), physical evidence for these structures is extremely rare. The Fountains buildings are fragmentary, in part destroyed by the construction of later stone buildings on the same site, but they tell us a great deal about Geoffroi and his instructions. Only the holes dug to take the principal posts of the walls have survived but many of the timbers

4 *Excavation has revealed traces of the first timber buildings at Fountains built in 1133 and visible only as the settings of timber posts beneath the foundations of the first stone church. The structure was built in the northern tradition with ground cills running between the vertical posts*

they contained had been sawn off at ground level when the buildings were taken down, allowing the stubs to rot away leaving a ghost of their shape in the ground. These ghosts could be measured; they were squared posts 0.4m across, set in straight lines, which indicates that the buildings were sophisticated, employing advanced carpentry. Indeed, Serlo has recorded for us the presence of carpenters and other workmen on site after the harvest of 1133, and they must have been responsible for the excavated buildings. Although the historian Orderic Vitalis records that the Cistercians 'have built their monasteries with their own labour' the evidence from Fountains is that they can have done little more than clear the site and provide unskilled labour.

The two buildings excavated can be identified as the core buildings of the reformed monastery: the church or oratory that lay east to west, and a domestic building that lay to its south west and parallel to it. Four bays of the church survived, 4.9m wide and at least 7.6m long, though both the east and west ends had been destroyed. Opposed doors were provided in the north and south walls in the westernmost surviving bay, with the door posts being set in pits outside the wall-lines suggesting shallow porches copying a known masonry prototype. The vertical posts were carefully aligned, and timber sill beams must have been fitted between them to hold the walls of wooden boards or staves. The roof must have been of thatch or shingles, for no trace of it was found in excavation. No internal fittings survived, though given the simplicity of the building the choir stalls may have been moveable benches. The domestic building appears to have been two-storeyed, although the only evidence for this was the greater depth of its post-pits.

The evidence of Clairvaux is critical here, for its timber buildings were still being used when Fountains was built (**6**). Although the church there has been destroyed, the domestic buildings are still standing in the western part of the precinct of the later monastery and were the subject of great interest in the seventeenth and eighteenth centuries as a monument to St Bernard. They appear on Dom Milley's great plan and perspective drawing of the abbey in the late eighteenth century, and are described in some detail by visitors in 1517 and 1667. The church lay to the south, was square in plan and was connected to a two-storey domestic building some 15m long, with the dormitory placed over the refectory. Between the dormitory and the church was a latrine building and a square room that contained the stair from the dormitory to the church. St Bernard's cell was at the top of the stair with a window looking down into the church. At the east end of the domestic range was a kitchen, identified by its half-round bread oven, and opposite that a suite of rooms for guests and the door keeper's chamber. Given that Geoffroi d'Ainai had lived in this building and was responsible for the laying out if not the actual building of the new monastery at Fountains, it is likely that he would have proposed something very similar which must lie below the north alley of the surviving cloister. It is interesting to note that Fountains did not subsequently use the Clairvaux layout for the temporary buildings of its own daughter-houses. The only documented example is at Meaux Abbey where Abbot Adam, one of the founding community at Fountains specifically trained for this purpose by Geoffroi d'Ainai in 1133, chose to place the oratory over the dormitory in late 1150. Abbot Robert of Newminster, the other monk trained by Geoffroi, chose to build two great aisled buildings at Sawley when he established his first daughter-house there in 1147 and both of these buildings have been located by excavation (**7**). It would appear that there was a steady development in the planning of temporary buildings that reflected

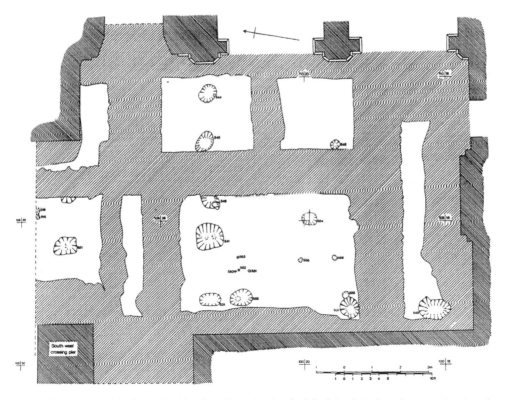

5 *The post-pits of the first timber church at Fountains (on the left of the plan) show the precise location of the timber wall-posts and double posts (**541**, **531**, & **521**) that mark shallow porches. Cross-hatching shows area where later buildings have destroyed the evidence for the earliest buildings*

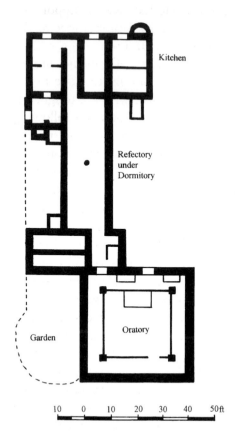

Kitchen

Refectory
under
Dormitory

Oratory

Garden

| 10 | 0 | 10 | 20 | 30 | 40 | 50ft |

6 *Plan of the first timber monastery at Clairvaux, redrawn and captioned, from Dom Milley's plan. Apart from the church, these buildings still survive in recognisable form*

the development of an architectural philosophy throughout the lifetime of St Bernard. In every case where such buildings are documented, they are described as being built 'according to the custom of the order'. The evidence for this development is starting to become clear within the extended family of Fountains.

Outside the Fountains family, the only other evidence for Cistercian temporary buildings in England comes from Bordesley Abbey. Here, the buildings have not been located on the ground, but timbers from them were used to cover early burials in the convent cemetery. Such was the significance of these early buildings to the community that the first monks took them to the grave. When temporary buildings were replaced in stone at Signy Abbey in the Ardennes, timbers not reused in the new buildings were ceremonially buried within the precinct, such was their symbolic importance to the community.

The threat of failure

The years 1133 and 1134 were a hard time for the Fountains community. Thurstan had only provided a minimal endowment of two carucates (about

105ha) at nearby Sutton and 81ha of the wood of Herleshowe to support the convent, compared with the seven carucates provided by Walter Espec at the founding of Rievaulx Abbey which had to support a community of the same size. Ricvaulx, being the first Cistercian house in the north of England, immediately attracted other endowments as local landowners sought to share in the spirituality of the men Serlo described as 'speaking on earth with the tongues of angels and who were most worthy of the name of monk'. Fountains following behind did not benefit from the same charity and failed to receive the support that would ensure *stabilitas*, the economic state required before the monastery could formally be accepted into the order. Not only did Fountains fail to attract gifts of land, it also failed to attract the recruits who flocked to Rievaulx. In the short term this was perhaps as well, for the harvest failed in 1133 while the temporary buildings were under construction, reducing the monks to a diet of gruel made from the leaves of their elm tree and field herbs. When Eustace FitzJohn of Knaresborough Castle sent a supply of bread to sustain the community who were on the verge of starvation, its remains were shared between the convent's workmen and the 'starving beggars at the gate'.

By 1134, it was apparent even to the founding community that their efforts must fail, and Abbot Richard went to the General Chapter at Cîteaux with a request to Abbot Bernard of Clairvaux that the community be allowed to abandon Fountains. Bernard reluctantly agreed to the request, and set aside his abbey's grange at Longué in the Haute Marne as a new home for the community.

On his return from Burgundy, Abbot Richard was to discover that the situation at Fountains had changed radically for the better, no doubt the result of Archbishop Thurstan's influence as founder. Hugh, Dean of Thurstan's cathedral

BUILDING A

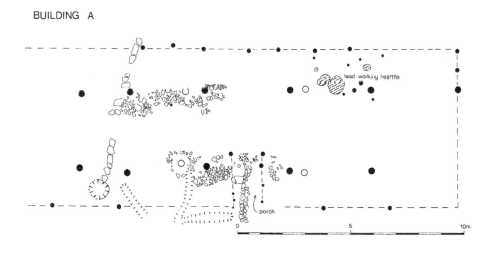

7 *One of the two aisled buildings constructed at Sawley Abbey in 1147-8 to house the monks while permanent buildings were constructed. The walls were of mud or clay, stiffened with slight timbers*

church and two more of its canons, another Serlo and Tosti, had chosen to retire to Fountains. All three, and particularly Hugh, were wealthy and brought their wealth and respectability with them. Additionally, Hugh brought his fine library to Fountains. The situation was saved, and the wealth brought by the three canons from York was put to the use of the convent. It was divided into three parts: the first was reserved in true Cistercian spirit for the poor; the second to establish a building fund; and the third part provided for the immediate needs of the community. Once the future appeared secure, endowments of land began to be offered (**8**). Robert de Sartis gave three carucates of land in the vill of Herleshowe to the south of the abbey, and Serlo de Pembroke, a kinsman of Eustace FitzJohn who had provided bread during the famine of 1133, gave two carucates of land at nearby Cayton. Further small states were given at Aldburgh and Warsill, the start of a process that was rapidly to gain momentum throughout the middle years of the twelfth century.

Security allowed the growth of the community, and by October 1135 when Abbot Richard successfully applied to the General Chapter for admission to the order he presided over a convent of 35 monks. Fountains was now equal to Rievaulx Abbey, a daughter-house of Clairvaux, charged with forwarding the Cistercian mission in England. With *stabilitas*, the time had come to build a permanent stone monastery, just as it had 29 years previously at Cîteaux.

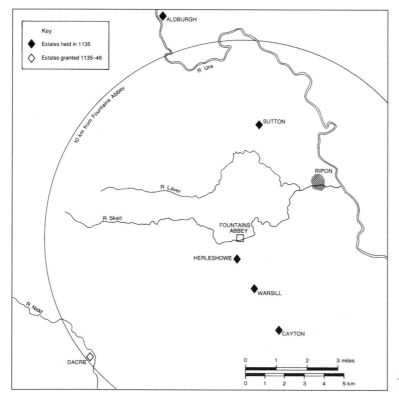

8 *The early estates were almost all to be found within 10km of the monastery*

2

THE FIRST STONE MONASTERY

The remarkable change of fortune that befell the Fountains community in 1135 marked the start of a period of sustained spiritual growth and financial security that was to continue well into the thirteenth century. Before his death in 1139, Abbot Richard was to see his convent established in a new stone church which was begun in 1136, one of the earliest known of the order's churches and built within 12 years of Bernard's *Apologia ad Gulielmum*. Its plan has been partially recovered by excavation and it represents the earliest form of stone church approved by so centralised an order.

Its building marks the second stage in the abbey's life, that of mission-centre responsible for spreading the Cistercian reform throughout England and further afield. The method by which the reform was spread was to dispatch groups of twelve monks and an abbot to establish daughter-houses on land given by patrons for that purpose. The abbot of each new daughter-house would normally be one of the most senior monks, and in the case of Fountains this meant members of the founding community trained by Geoffroi d'Ainai. The ability to establish colonies was strictly controlled by the availability of monks and the availability of willing patrons, and the events of the late 1130s demonstrate that Fountains' growing reputation attracted both many recruits to the cloister and men of substance who were sufficiently impressed to endow new monasteries. In this, Fountains was to outshine Rievaulx.

The first colonies

The first daughter-house established from Fountains in 1138 was settled on the fen-edge in Lincolnshire at Haverholme near Sleaford (**9**). The first abbot was Gervase, one of the founding monks from York. A party of lay brothers had been sent to Haverholme the previous year to prepare the site, evidence that Fountains had begun to recruit the *conversi* who were to establish the agricultural fortunes of the house, as well as choir monks. The site was provided by Bishop Alexander 'the Magnificent' of Lincoln, a certain sign that the community in Skelldale had achieved spiritual respectability. Alexander had almost certainly been introduced to the Fountains community by Archbishop Thurstan and he was to remain a

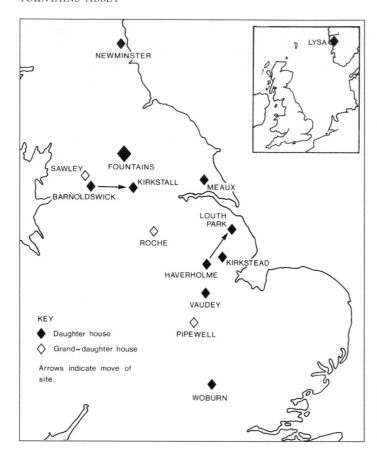

9 *The daughter-houses and grand-daughter-houses of Fountains in England and Norway*

committed supporter of the Cistercians in his vast diocese that extended from the Thames to the Humber. It appears that this first daughter-house was founded more from piety than practicality and the site proved to be unsuitable, a common problem with many Cistercian colonies, and Bishop Alexander moved the community to a new site in his deer-park at Louth, from which the new abbey became known as *de Parco Ludo* or Louth Park Abbey.

A second colony was dispatched to the wilds of Northumberland under the abbacy of Robert, the ex-Whitby monk who was one of the first Fountains community. The name given to this new daughter-house is significant for it was called *Novum Monasterium* or Newminster, the original name of Cîteaux itself. Its temporary buildings were laid out by Abbot Robert himself 'after our manner' though the founder, Ranulph de Merlay, lord of Morpeth, claimed responsibility for their construction. This split responsibility was to ensure that suitable buildings were erected before the new colony arrived, a requirement of Cistercian statutes since at least 1113.

The planning of new colonies took some time as the foundation of the third daughter-house, of Kirkstead in Lincolnshire, proves. Hugh Brito, the lord of

Tattershall, had visited Fountains in 1137 but two years were spent preparing the site before Robert of Subella and twelve monks were sent out to settle it. Not only were buildings and monks required for a new foundation, but the statutes of the order required that each new colony was to be sent out with its complement of necessary and officially approved books: a missal, the gospels, a gradual, an antiphonary, a hymnal, a psalter, a copy of the rule, and a religious calendar. Because these books had to reflect the Cistercian reform they would have to be copied at the mother-house, a lengthy process in itself. Since the initial foundation of Fountains itself had been so uncertain, careful planning seems to have gone hand-in-hand with religious zeal for not one of the eight colonies established from Fountains before 1150 was to fail.

By the death of Abbot Richard, the establishment of daughter-houses had depleted the Fountains community of a quarter of its original members, 36 choir monks who had joined the first community, and an unknown number of lay brothers. In the same period, Rievaulx, Fountains' natural rival, had established two colonies, both in 1136. In both cases there seems to have been a direct correlation between the number of recruits to the mother-house and the need to establish colonies, as though the intention was to keep the mother-house to a manageable size. This is reflected at Fountains in the stone church built by Abbot Richard.

A stone church

The earliest stone churches of the Cistercians, those of Cîteaux and Pontigny, known only from contemporary descriptions, were rectangular buildings of great simplicity, a far cry from the monumental church begun at Clairvaux by the architects Achard and Geoffroi d'Ainai in 1135 and which is now seen as the model for the order's twelfth century churches. The contemporary church built at Fountains is more typical of the order's early churches, cruciform but with an unstressed crossing, a short square-ended presbytery to house the altar, and small rectangular transept chapels. Only the south transept and parts of the crossing and presbytery have been excavated, but sufficient has been seen to indicate its likely plan (**4** & **10**).

The new church enveloped the site of the timber oratory, an unusual feature for its building must have interfered with the constant round of services. Normally, a replacement church would have been built on an adjacent site to avoid this inconvenience, but at Fountains the site of the community's first church was deemed to be so important that it was to be reused by succeeding churches. More remarkable, though, than the placing of this church was its scale. It was small, and unlike its successors it had a short and unaisled nave, and the transepts were mere adjuncts, walled off from the main body of the church. It was not built for a large community and must simply have been

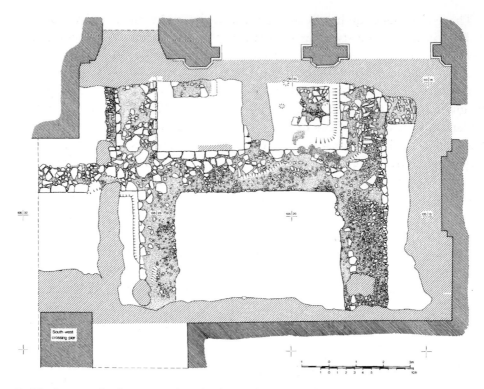

10 *The first stone church survives only as foundations, for its materials were reused to build its successor. Only the south transept and a part of the crossing have been excavated*

intended to serve only for the mission phase of the house when the choir monks cannot have numbered more than 40 or 50. Even so, the church must have seemed distinctly cramped. The lack of a large aisled nave precluded the army of lay brothers that became a later feature of the house.

The plan of the church is comparable with the other early churches known at Waverley in Surrey, a grand-daughter of Cîteaux founded in 1128 and built presumably in the early 1130s, and Tintern, founded from Waverley in 1131 (**11**). Nothing survives of the superstructure of the Fountains church but comparison with surviving fabric at Waverley shows that the building was tall and apparently reflected the architecture of the Burgundian cradle of the order. Some indication of the height of the transepts at Fountains can be gained from the later buildings that abutted them. While it respected the Cistercian philosophy of simplicity, the inspiration for the church's plan can have come from non-Cistercian sources, particularly the simple churches of the Augustinian canons who had spread through England a generation before the Cistercians arrived. Similar form and scale can be detected at Porchester Priory, built with royal support in the years after 1133, the simple church of Kirkham priory built in the 1120s, or the small Benedictine church at Ewenny, built in the 1130s but not actually colonised before 1141.

The Fountains church tells us a great deal about the community that built it. First it was a free-standing structure without an associated cloister, with timber domestic buildings to its south that replaced the original domestic range. Though these buildings have yet to be discovered, they must have been similar to the second phase of timber buildings excavated at Fountains' grand-daughter-house of Sawley, raised in the 1170s (**12**). Secondly, it betrays evidence of the community's Benedictine origins, both in plan and decoration. The east end of the building was built to a stepped plan, with the inner transept chapels being deeper than the outer ones. Although the chapels and presbytery are square-ended, their plan repeats the stepped apses that marked the east end of the twelfth-century York Abbey, perhaps an unconscious repetition of the design of the church the monks had previously known. Like York Abbey, the church had been plastered and painted internally and externally. Most of this plaster was white-limed and overpainted with a masonry pattern common to all orders in the twelfth century. However, a respond capital from one of the arches into a transept chapel had survived and been reset in the lower walling of the later church, and this retained traces of multi-coloured leaf decoration that was very un-Cistercian in its appearance. Glass, too, survived from the windows of the south transept chapels, and this was not the plain glass favoured by the order and mandatory from 1147 but included red and blue quarries that implied decorated windows. The simplicity of the order was expressed in different ways. The altars in the transept chapels were simple affairs built of

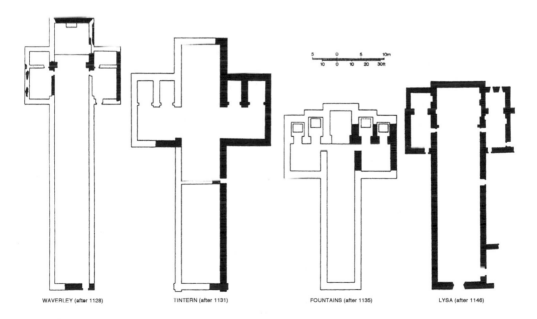

WAVERLEY (after 1128)   TINTERN (after 1131)   FOUNTAINS (after 1135)   LYSA (after 1146)

11 *A reconstructed plan of the first stone church at Fountains compared with other early Cistercian churches at Waverley, Tintern and Lysa*

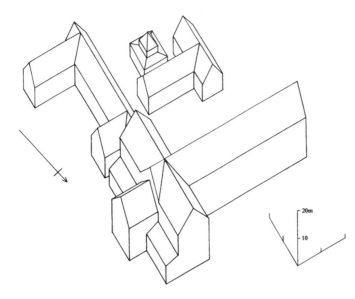

12 *The second phase of timber buildings at Sawley comprised a dormitory over a refectory, a kitchen, and a guest hall, contemporary with the first phase of a stone church and the construction (but probably not the use) of the east cloister range. The new timber buildings at Fountains must have been similar*

wood and set in the plain mortar floors of the chapels. The main body of the transept had an earth floor, while the more important areas of the choir and presbytery had mortar floors, separated by a single step that marked the entrance to the presbytery. The choir stalls, of which no trace remained, were set against the walls that closed off the transepts, and between them the floor was strewn with compressed layers of rushes.

Abbot Richard was replaced by his prior, another Richard who had been the sacrist at York, a saintly man who felt himself to be unworthy of his promotion and shrank from the administrative duties of his office. He was deeply respected by the community for his religious conviction and ability to resolve spiritual problems. He was not the person to involve himself with great building schemes, and between 1139 and his death in 1143 Fountains enjoyed a period of consolidation. During his abbacy, Archbishop Thurstan died, depriving the community of its founder and principal patron, and the second Abbot Richard was to involve the abbey in a dispute over his successor that was to have disastrous consequences in later years.

In 1144, Abbot Bernard of Clairvaux intervened in the affairs of Fountains to provide a strong leader who would impress Cistercian orthodoxy on the convent that still retained traces of its Benedictine past. Henry Murdac, abbot of Vauclair on the Somme, was sent to Fountains ostensibly to advise the community on the choice of a new abbot but in reality to be elected himself. A Yorkshireman by birth and one-time master of the Schools in York, he had taught Abbot William of Rievaulx before both had entered Clairvaux.

Henry was a close friend of Bernard, and Clairvaux-trained and a zealot to the point of being overbearing, he was just the person to ensure the strengthening of the abbey, being the first abbot trained in continental practice. Murdac was a builder, he had just seen the rebuilding of the church and cloister at Clairvaux, and as abbot of Vauclair had been responsible for building the church there on the Clairvaux model. At Fountains he was to complete the building of the first stone monastery, and was indirectly responsible for its destruction by fire in 1146.

Abbot Henry's buildings

Murdac must have been appalled by what he found at Fountains on his arrival in 1144. The small church and timber domestic buildings represented an outdated philosophy, for the Cistercians on the continent had moved back to the principles of un-reformed Benedictine planning that had been abandoned by the founding generation. The reason for this was simply growing numbers and the success of the reform movement. The order had taken the standard Benedictine layout (**13**) and modified it to their own needs and taste. Gone was the informal layout of simple buildings, to be replaced by the formal enclosure of the cloister. The presence of lay brothers required a departure from the Benedictine plan, for

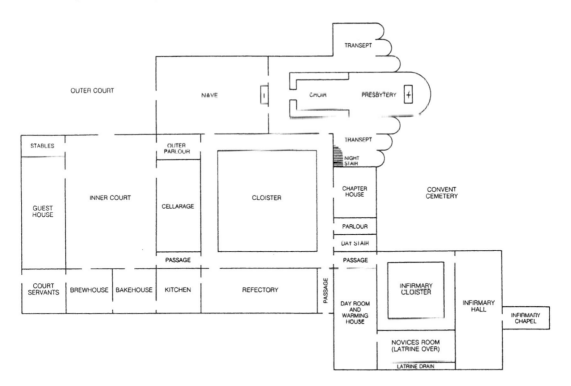

13 *The ground plan of a typical Benedictine monastery in the first half of the twelfth century differed little from that of the St Gall plan of the early ninth century. The living accommodation of the monks was placed around a square cloister with the church normally on the north side. The dormitory occupied the first floor of the east range, and the abbot's house the first floor of the west range. Compare with* **14A**

their accommodation was to be separate from that of the choir monks, and they were to have their own church. Their presence also required the provision of an outer court within the monastery where they could work, separated again from the monks to emphasise their secondary status.

Murdac's primary task was therefore to enlarge the first stone church and build permanent cloister buildings of the latest continental design for the community (**14**). What is immediately apparent about Murdac's building is its scale. A vast cloister was laid out to the south of the existing church, 38m square, contemporary with the addition of a great aisled nave to Abbot Richard's small church. This cloister survives today. Considerable parts of Murdac's cloister ranges, the house he built for the community, also still survives, embedded in later buildings. Enough remains above ground or has been excavated over the past 30 years to reconstruct not only the plan of his monastery, but also to recover details of its elevations (**15**). His buildings, which were completed in less than three years, can be recognised by their distinctive masonry (**16**). Parts of the east, south, and west cloister ranges survive to their full height of 6.10m, capped by a chamfered string-course that carried the eaves of the roof. Excavation has demonstrated that all of the buildings were roofed in tile. The ranges were 7m wide internally, the same width as the earliest cloister ranges recently identified at Rievaulx, a fact that might suggest modular planning that has already been detected in early Cistercian churches. These new and closely dated cloister buildings provide the finest example of early twelfth-century planning in the order and demonstrate best

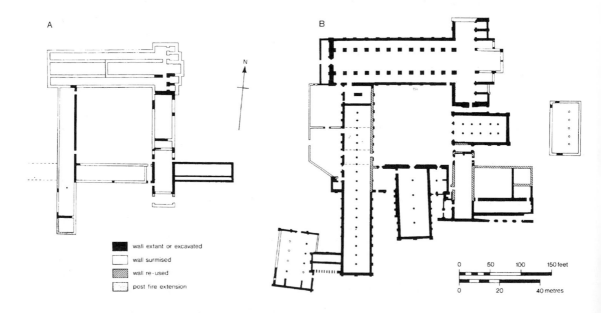

wall extant or excavated
wall surmised
wall re-used
post fire extension

14 *The ground plan of Abbot Henry's monastery (A) has been identified by studying the standing remains and by excavation. Its buildings largely remain within the surviving buildings of the late twelfth century monastery (B) built by Abbots Richard of Clairvaux and Robert of Pipewell*

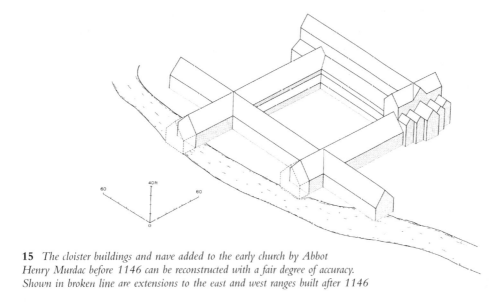

15 *The cloister buildings and nave added to the early church by Abbot
Henry Murdac before 1146 can be reconstructed with a fair degree of accuracy.
Shown in broken line are extensions to the east and west ranges built after 1146*

continental practice that must have been derived from Clairvaux itself, where the
early twelfth-century buildings have been largely destroyed.

Before any building could be contemplated, the River Skell was moved
some 26m (84ft) to the south, and a stone-lined drain was built along its old
line to flush the latrines that were to be built to serve both the lay brothers in
the west range and choir monks in the east range of the new cloister. Next a
terrace was created on the valley floor, approximately level with the floor of
Abbot Richard's church. On this terrace the new cloister buildings were raised.
The east range was butted up to the south transept of the existing church, but
the contemporary west range was bonded with the south wall of the extended
nave, showing that it had to be a part of Abbot Henry's work.

The east range was of two storeys, and still survives at its south end to full
height. Against the south transept of the church was the chapter-house where
the abbey's business was conducted, discipline enforced, and a daily chapter of
the rule of St Benedict heard. It was contained within the range and must have
been a low, dark room, for its ceiling was the wooden floor of the dormitory
above that was only 2.14m (7ft) above ground level. To the south of the
chapter-house was the parlour, the only room in the cloister where conversa-
tion was allowed. Next came the day-stair to the dormitory, approached by a
tall door (now blocked) from the cloister. The stair itself must have been of
timber for it has left no trace, and there was a tiny room below the stair, lit by
a round-headed window that still survives (**108**). To the south of the day-stair
was a passage through the range, and to the south of this the day-room set aside
for manual work within the cloister. In a Benedictine monastery this room
would have been provided with fireplaces and doubled as the warming-house

16 *Part of Henry Murdac's east range survives to full height encased within a later rebuilding. It can be identified by its small, roughly squared blocks of gritstone with wide mortar joints, the remains of thick external wall plaster, and the total lack of any decoration*

where fires were permitted between 1 November and Good Friday, but at Fountains there is no evidence that this room was heated at all, a certain indication that Cistercian life was meant to be hard and unremitting.

To the east of the east range was a long building partially set over the original course of the Skell. Its upper floor was the monks' latrine, communicating with their dormitory by a door which still survives and to the north of which is the round-headed opening in which a lamp was placed to light access to the latrine at night. Its ground floor had a long narrow room walled off from the latrine drain, traditionally the space set aside for the training of novices. Latrine chutes in the thickness of its south wall served a yard between this building and the river Skell, an area set aside for manual work outside the cloister buildings. All monasteries took sanitation seriously, but none more so than the Cistercians, and the latrine drain was constantly flushed with running water, ensuring that sewage was flushed away and the risk of disease minimised.

The upper floor of the east range, the monks' dormitory, was lit by a series of small, round-headed windows and was an undivided space 49m long. The monks' beds were ranged along the side walls, allowing space for about 70 choir monks. Night access to the church was provided by a door in the gable wall of the south transept, but the principal access was by the day-stair from the east cloister alley.

The south range of the cloister contained the refectory, aligned west to east and open to the roof in the same manner as a domestic hall. Only a fragment of its north wall survives to full height, showing that the south range was the same height as the other ranges. At the east end of the refectory was a passage through the range, the south door of which still survives, leading to a yard on the south side of the refectory, a standard provision in twelfth-century Benedictine cloisters. There was a room above the passage accessible from the monks' dormitory, almost certainly a private chamber for the abbot who lived in common with his monks and was required by statute to sleep within the dormitory. St Bernard had a private chamber off the dormitory in the first monastery at Clairvaux and it is tempting to see this as evidence for the gradual separation of the abbot from the community that became much more obvious in the second half of the twelfth century.

The west range was the home of the lay brothers and with the exception of the chapter-house it mirrored the accommodation provided for the monks, an open dormitory 64m long at first-floor level, large enough to house perhaps 140 lay brethren. The ground floor comprised several rooms but the partition walls, which were of timber, have not been traced. At the north end was the outer parlour where members of the community could receive visitors from the outside world. Its door to the cloister survives, blocked in the 1150s. Towards the centre of the range was cellarage, extending most of the length of the cloister. South of this was a passage through the range, flanked by a cubicle for the porter in the thickness of the east wall next to the door that provided access to the cloister alleys. Immediately to the south of this, the remainder of the range was taken up by the lay brothers' refectory, so placed to share the kitchen in the south range of the cloister. Unlike the tall monks' refectory, the lay brothers' dining room was a low building; an offset in the east wall of the range indicates that the dormitory floor was only 2.1m above ground floor level. The lay brothers' latrine, still unexcavated, lay above the old course of the Skell to the west of their refectory. The east and west ranges extended to within 6m of the north bank of the realigned river and in a yard between them would have been a detached kitchen, probably served by a bridge across the Skell. A metalled path has been located, skirting the south end of the west range and leading into the kitchen yard.

Of Murdac's enlargement of the church, only a short length of its south aisle wall can be seen in the floor at the north end of the surviving west range. It indicates that the nave was extended substantially to the west, the intention being to provide space for a church for the lay brothers. Aisles were necessary as passages to provide access since the main body of the church was divided into liturgical units by screens. To establish the likely plan of Murdac's new nave it is necessary to look at the church he built at Vauclair (**17**) before he came to Fountains, because the nave at Fountains has not been excavated.

The abbey of Vauclair was founded in 1134 and permanent buildings were begun within a year or two of settlement and it is likely that construction of the church was completed before Murdac's departure for Fountains in 1144. Abbot Henry's church was unknown before its excavation in the late 1960s. Only the

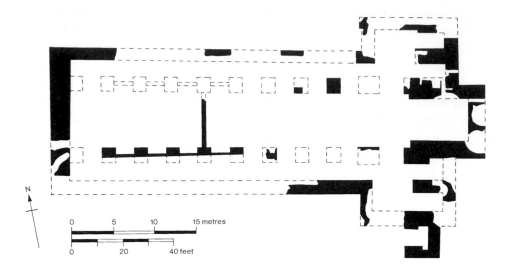

17 *Ground plan of Henry Murdac's church at Vauclair, one of the earliest known churches of the family of Clairvaux, built shortly before he became abbot of Fountains in 1144.* After René Courtois and la Groupe Sources

18 *The abbey church at Fontenay, conventionally dated to before 1147 but probably slightly later, remains complete, demonstrating the simplicity of the 'Bernardine' model.* Terryl Kinder

foundations had survived a later rebuilding but the plan they demonstrate is the earliest known example of 'Bernardine' planning derived from the great church of Clairvaulx itself. The two churches must in fact be closely contemporary in date. The nave of nine bays is what concerns us here, for its dimensions bear a remarkable resemblance to the dimensions of Murdac's nave at Fountains which must have been modelled closely on it. Its appearance is unknown, but another contemporary church, that of the Clairvaux colony of Fontenay, remains intact. Built between 1139 and 1147, it is closely contemporary with Murdac's churches and its stark Burgundian detailing with pointed arches to the main arcades might give a clue as to the appearance of the Fountains nave (**18**). Unlike Fontenay, Fountains appears to have had an upper storey lighting its nave, and it would have been roofed in timber and not vaulted. This was the model favoured at Clairvaux and the lack of a clerestory at Fontenay may simply be a mark of lower status within the order.

The destruction of Fountains in 1146

Abbot Richard II had involved his abbey in the disputed election of William FitzHerbert to the archbishopric of York in 1140. King Stephen had nominated William to the see against the united opposition of the Augustinians and Cistercians who did not consider him to be a suitable candidate. With the support of Bernard of Clairvaux, Richard took the case to Rome and persuaded Pope Eugenius III, himself a Cistercian monk, to withhold recognition of the election. Richard died at Clairvaux on his return journey and his successor, Abbot Henry, no doubt instructed by St Bernard, took up the fight with his customary zeal. Henry himself soon became the favoured candidate of the opposition party, bringing accusations of simony (the purchase of church office) against the archbishop at the Council of Rheims that were to lead to his deposition early in 1147.

So intense was the antagonism in 1146 that supporters of Archbishop William marched on Fountains seeking to murder Abbot Henry. Unable to find him, they sacked the abbey, finding little of value in the process, and fired its buildings. Serlo, who was present during the attack, tells how 'the convent stood by and saw the buildings erected by the sweat of their brows enveloped in flames and soon to be ashes, and that only the oratory and offices adjoining it reserved for prayer remained half-consumed, like a brand plucked from the burning', a slight exaggeration to judge from what survives. Excavation has proved, however, that his overall description of the events was reasonably accurate. Traces of a serious fire have been found in both the east and west cloister ranges and in the south transept of the church itself, where the burning was sufficiently severe to melt the window glass (**19**) and bring down the wall-plaster. Henry Murdac himself had been in the church during the assault, prostrated before the high altar, and

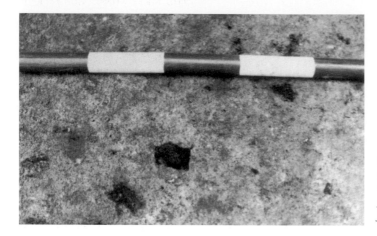

19 *Intense burning in the south chapel of the south transept left melted window glass and fallen wall plaster fused to the mortar floor*

it is significant that no trace of burning was found in the choir and presbytery, where the rushes on the floor were not even charred. The wall that separated the transept from the crossing had evidently contained the fire, and miraculously the abbey church survived in a usable state.

FitzHerbert's deposition in 1147 left the way clear for Abbot Henry's election to the archbishopric, though King Stephen refused to invest him with the temporalities of the see and feeling ran so strongly against him that he was unable to enter his own cathedral city. It was a pyrrhic victory that had cost his convent their home and forced him to administer his archdiocese from the bishop's palace at Ripon that the founding community had left with such hopes on 27 December 1132.

Reconstruction

Henry Murdac was obliged to resign his abbacy when he became archbishop, though he continued to impose his will on two of his successors. The first was Maurice, who had previously been the second abbot of Rievaulx, and before he joined the Cistercians there he had been sub-prior of the great cathedral priory of Durham. After three months he retired again to Rievaulx, finding his position intolerable, to be succeeded by another Rievaulx monk, Thorold, who later became abbot of Trois-Fontaines. To Thorold fell the task of rebuilding the ruined abbey. In Serlo's words the monks 'repaired the fallen places and rebuilt the ruins, and as it was written: 'the walls had fallen but were rebuilt with squared stones''. The south transept of the church was refitted, with new mortar floors and stone altars in the eastern chapels which sealed the evidence of burning (**20**). The cloister ranges must have been roofless shells, and a grant of timber from Alan earl of Richmond in 1147 might be associated with the replacement of burned floors and roofs. It is impossible to tell from what remains if more drastic reconstruction was required. The opportu-

20 *A new stone altar set on the burned mortar floor replaced the burned wooden altar in the northern transept chapel when the building was restored after the fire of 1146*

nity was taken during the post-fire repair to extend both the east and west ranges (the extensions are shown on **15** as broken lines), extending both the lay brothers' and monks' dormitories to allow for growing numbers as well as providing additional room at ground-floor level. The replacement of the wooden floor to the lay brothers' dormitory with a stone vault supported on masonry piers had the effect of fire-proofing the ground floor.

The second phase of colonisation

Abbot Henry continued the policy of missionary colonisation begun by Abbot Richard when he persuaded Hugh de Bolbec to endow a daughter-house at Woburn in Bedfordshire in 1145 (see fig. **9**). The colony was led by Alan, one of the founding community, and additionally brother Adam was again employed to set out the temporary buildings. Although Adam was used regularly for this task, it is unknown what his contribution was to the development of Fountains, for he was there throughout Abbot Henry's building campaign and Abbot Thorold's reconstruction. Serlo makes no mention of him in this context.

Following the destruction of Fountains by FitzHerbert's supporters, three more daughter-houses were settled in 1146-7, the number suggesting the need to reduce the size of the mother-community while repairs were carried out. The first of these in 1146 demonstrates the internationalism of the Cistercians. Led by Ranulf, a colony set out for Norway, settling at Lysa near Bergen at the invitation of Bishop Sigurd who had visited Fountains and provided the site. Clairvaux had already settled a daughter-house at Alvastra in Sweden in 1143, and the settlement of Lysakloster from Fountains suggests a policy within the Clairvaux family to bring the Cistercian mission to Scandinavia, planned by St Bernard himself. In 1147, monks from Fountains daughter-house of Kirkstead were settled at Hovedö, and Lysa itself established a daughter-house at Tutterö in 1207, completing the Cistercian settlement of Norway within the Fountains family.

The second colony set out in March to settle at Barnoldswick in Craven under the patronage of two powerful Yorkshire barons, William de Poitou and Henry de Lacy. Led by Alexander, the party of twelve monks included Serlo who by this time would have been one of the senior members of the Fountains community. The site at Barnoldswick was not an ideal one: it proved too wet and was based on a pre-existing settlement that did not provide the detachment from the world that the Cistercian statutes required. Abbot Alexander's demolition of the parish church did little to improve relations with the local community, and the convent moved to a better site at Kirkstall in the Aire valley to the west of Leeds on the advice of their patrons in 1152.

The third colony was led by Warin, exceptionally not one of the monks from York, and set out for Bytham in Lincolnshire where a site had been granted by William le Gros, count of Aumâle and earl of Yorkshire. Like Barnoldswick this site proved unsatisfactory, this time having too little water, and in 1149 the convent moved to a new site provided by one of William's tenants that they called *Vallis Dei*, the Valley of God, and which became known in English as Vaudey. Here, the abbey buildings were again laid out by brother Adam. The failure of both initial sites suggests that they were chosen too hurriedly, supporting the suggestion that that monks were being removed from Fountains because of the abbey's destruction rather than in a carefully planned policy of colonisation.

Planned during the reconstruction of Fountains and settled late in 1150 was an eighth and final colony at Meaux in Holderness. Brother Adam had met William le Gros in 1149 when he was engaged in laying out the buildings of Vaudey and had been asked to advise the count how he could redeem a pledge made in his youth to go on pilgrimage to the Holy Land that he could no longer undertake because he had grown too old and fat. He was already the patron of three monasteries including Vaudey. Brother Adam suggested the foundation of a second Cistercian abbey, and Pope Eugenius III readily agreed to a dispensation of his vow. Adam was to lead the colony himself and William invited him to choose a site on his extensive estates. He chose, to the count's distress, the land in Holderness 'well planted with woods and orchards, surrounded with rivers and waters and favoured with rich soil' that William had recently purchased and was in the process of enclosing as a deer-park.

The establishment of Meaux Abbey ended the first generation of the Fountains family. A second generation was also growing, for Newminster under its first abbot, St Robert, had established colonies of its own: at Pipewell in Northamptonshire in 1143, and at Roche in south Yorkshire and Sawley in Craven in 1147. In England the Fountains family was complete and the mission phase was over. From 1150, Fountains was to be transformed from a missionary outpost to the head of a substantial family of subsidiary monasteries, like Clairvaux a mother-house at the head of its own filiation.

3

FOUNTAINS – THE MOTHER-HOUSE

The removal of Abbot Thorold in 1150 marked a watershed in the history of Fountains for it coincided with the end of the mission phase of the house. Urged by Archbishop Henry, St Bernard returned Thorold to Rievaulx for he had proved to be too independent. In his place Bernard imposed an excellent candidate, Richard of Clairvaux, a native of York like Murdac and Abbot William of Rievaulx, and a man of great austerity trained in the best continental Cistercian practice. He had risen to be precentor at Clairvaux and followed Murdac as Abbot of Vauclair.

The new Abbot Richard, formally elected in 1151, had the difficult job of keeping the peace with Archbishop Henry until his death in 1153 and arranging a reconciliation with Archbishop William FitzHerbert thereafter. William in his turn became a good friend of Fountains, visiting in May 1154 and promising financial support for building work then in hand. The ending of the 13 year-old dispute in turn allowed Fountains to recover from the disturbed and weakened state the feud had caused, and before the abbot's death in 1170 the Augustinian canon William of Newburgh was to describe Fountains, together with Rievaulx and Byland, as one of the 'three shining lights' of northern monasticism. All three had exceptional abbots at the time who were all great builders.

Recovery and growing numbers no longer relieved by the foundation of daughter-houses resulted in a cramped community, for Murdac's cloister buildings were too small for the number of monks and lay brothers who flocked to the abbey. As the head of a good-sized family, Fountains also enjoyed an enhanced status within the order and required rather grander buildings than it possessed to demonstrate this. Abbot Richard III began a campaign of building that was to continue into the last decade of the twelfth century, transforming his abbey from a simple daughter-house of Clairvaux to the mother-house of a substantial *familia* (**14B**).

A great stone church

First to be built, or at least begun, was a monumental new church (**colour plate 1**), which was started within a few years of Abbot Richard's election and

21 *Abbot Aelred's church at Rievaulx of which the nave and transepts remain provided the basic design for the new church at Fountains begun by Abbot Richard of Clairvaux*

probably occasioned Archbishop William's visit in 1154. Its inspiration came not directly from France but from nearby Rievaulx, where a similar church had been begun perhaps five years earlier by the very English abbot, St Aelred, for his rapidly growing community. The rebuilding of the church at Fountains was to begin a rivalry of building campaigns that was to last well into the following century. Rivalry was not only expressed in buildings, but also in the religious zeal that drew recruits. Under Aelred, Rievaulx grew to house at least 500 lay brothers and 150 choir monks. Fountains was never to achieve numbers like these, for even at their greatest extent its cloister buildings could not have housed more than 120 monks and 400 lay brethren.

A great deal remains of Aelred's church at Rievaulx or was recovered by excavation in the early 1920s (**21**). Burgundian in style, it conforms to the 'Bernardine' plan of the great church at Clairvaux itself. The church at Rievaulx was the first large Cistercian church to be built in England, with an aisled nave of nine bays and a two-storeyed elevation. Its transepts survive to full height and sufficient remains of its nave to be sure of its design (**22A**). Detailing was severe, almost to the point of non-existence, the piers and pointed arches of the nave being boldly chamfered but lacking any mouldings and rising from square bases. The roughly-coursed rubble that made up the walls was plastered, white-limed, and lined out in white paint to resemble good quality masonry. The nave aisles were transversely vaulted, carrying the profiles of the nave arcades back to the aisle walls, a feature seen at Fontenay, designed to support the thrust of a high vault. The nave was not vaulted, however, but roofed in wood. In this, Rievaulx belongs to an early group of great Cistercian churches best represented by the church of Clermont in Normandy built in the 1150s.

Although the model for the new church at Fountains was undoubtedly Aelred's church at Rievaulx its design marked a significant development in Cistercian architecture. Its plan and two storey elevation were definitely taken from Rievaulx, but its architectural detailing was not (**22B** & **23**). Instead, this was developed separately using details first seen in England at Sawley Abbey, a grand-daughter of Fountains begun after 1147 and almost certainly the direct inspiration for the design of Fountains itself (**24**).

The church at Fountains, though starkly devoid of decoration, was meant from the first to demonstrate the wealth and importance of the abbey and like the great church at Clairvaux was built to a scale that was out of keeping with the simplicity urged in St Bernard's *Apologia*. In this it went further than the Rievaulx church, for though it was built for a smaller community it was significantly longer, having a nave of eleven bays, and was built throughout of finely cut ashlar masonry, though it was white-limed and painted in exactly the same way as Rievaulx. Building exclusively in carefully cut masonry, even though the quarry was adjacent to the church, was slow and costly, and it is hardly

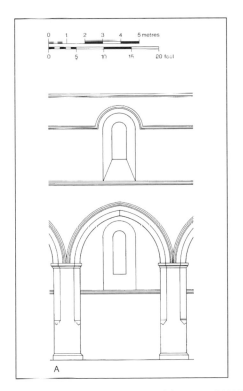
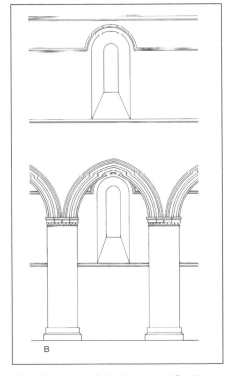

22 *Comparative bay elevations of the naves of (A) Rievaulx,* after Harrison *and (B) Fountains.* After Reeve

surprising that the *narratio* records that it was not completed for some 20 years. It says, with characteristic understatement, that it rose 'far more lavish' than its small predecessor. The period of its building falls conveniently between Bernard of Clairvaux's death in 1153 and his canonisation in 1174.

The new church has a complicated structural history caused partly by its being built around its predecessor so far as was practicable. The reason for this was the constant need for a church to house the altar and in which the community could sing the seven daily offices and celebrate Mass. The first parts to be built were the presbytery, transepts and crossing (**23**), requiring the demolition of the same parts of the earlier church. Although Richard of Clairvaux's presbytery was later demolished, his transepts with their eastern chapels remain virtually intact (**colour plate 6**). The tall pointed arches into the chapels are simply relieved by chamfering and have neither bases or capitals. Above there is blank walling capped by tall round-headed windows. The church was intentionally tall and austere with a distinct Burgundian flavour. Originally, the crossing was designed simply as a continuation of the nave up to the entrance to the presbytery, without a central tower at the intersection.

23 *The earliest surviving work in the church at Fountains is found in the south transept and its eastern chapels.* English Heritage

24 *The eastern transept arcade and chapels at Sawley Abbey, built around 1150, are almost certainly the source for the transept design at Fountains.* Rich Williams

25 *Excavation has revealed that the southern arcade of the nave overlies the foundations of the west wall of the transept which runs across the south aisle, showing that the nave was originally designed without an aisle.*

The nave, which demonstrates a radical change in design, was not built at the same time as the transepts, but shortly after. Excavation (**25**) has shown that the nave was originally intended to be unaisled like the church at Sawley that it copies, and the foundations of the west walls of the transepts run across the ends of the later nave aisles. There is no indication that this nave was ever begun and Murdac's nave was probably left in place until the eastern parts of the church were completed. Only when the eastern parts of the new church were substantially complete could it be demolished and a new nave built. A clue to the sequence of events is the door leading into the new nave from the east walk of the cloister (**26**). It is almost certainly re-used from Murdac's nave

26 *The processional door from the cloister dates to the 1140s and is probably re-used from Henry Murdac's church*

as is much of the facing stone of the south aisle wall which, particularly on its inner face, is of poorer quality than the ashlar used elsewhere in Abbot Richard III's work.

The transept of the new church was linked to the existing east range by a rebuilt section of the range that intruded into the original chapter-house and which contained a library and sacristy on its ground floor with the truncated northern part of the dormitory above. This rebuilding was carried up only to the height of the existing east range. Quite clearly, the intention was only to add a new church to Murdac's cloister at this stage, and this is confirmed by two features in the south transept gable. The first of these is the provision of two windows at clerestory level which were placed to clear the east range roof. The second was a night-stair provided from the new church to the old dormitory. Because the new church was built on a raised terrace 1m above its predecessor, the floor of the dormitory was only 1.52m above the transept floor. A tall door at the floor level of the church was incorporated in the south wall of the transept, through which a short stairway provided the necessary access.

When work began on the rebuilding of the nave in the late 1150s, provision was made for a central tower. Towers had originally been forbidden by the General Chapter but that proscription had begun to weaken as Cistercian architecture continued to develop. In 1157, the General Chapter amended the statutes to the effect that 'stone towers with bells [are] not [to] be built'. The crossing tower at Fountains was not a bell-tower but a lantern to throw light into the choir area, the heart of the church, and it is highly significant that the early Cistercians saw light as a manifestation of the Holy Spirit.

The new nave marked a second stage, therefore, in the design of the great church and it is fortunate that it survives virtually in the state that it was built (**27**). It was constructed in sections though it represents a unified design. The eastern four bays which housed the choir-monks were the first to be built. These supported the crossing and its new tower and were presumably closed off at the west end with a temporary timber screen on the line of the later rood screen. The footings of the whole structure must have been laid out when the work was begun, for the next part of the church to be built was the west front and the four western bays that overlapped Murdac's west range. The south aisle wall was constructed to close off the cloister. Work was then temporarily abandoned, and was not resumed until the 1170s when Abbot Robert of Pipewell completed the church and provided a choir for the lay brethren.

The nave maintained the two-storey elevation of the transepts, and was very clearly modelled on Rievaulx (**22B**), both in plan and elevation, though it demonstrates a remarkable development in only a few years. The Fountains nave is taller and better proportioned, and the harshness of the Rievaulx design

27 *The late twelfth century nave which contained the lay brothers' choir, is little altered since it was built. Only the west window, inserted in 1494, would not be recognised by its builders*

28 *Decoration, unknown at Rievaulx, can be seen on the scalloped and waterleaf capitals of the nave piers and on the corbels that carry the transverse arches of the aisle vaults.* English Heritage

has been lost. Although it is still an austere building, decoration has begun to appear (**28**). Cylindrical piers rose from moulded bases and were capped by scalloped capitals that carried moulded arcades of two orders, and the corbels that carried the transverse arches across the aisles were decorated with fine Anglo-Norman leaf detail. As at Rievaulx, the nave aisles were provided with transverse vaults and the main span had a wooden roof which was boarded in to provide the impression of a vault. The line of this timber ceiling can still be seen in the profile of the arch on the inner face of the west gable wall (**27**).

The original design of the west front, built about 1160, can be reconstructed. Across the width of the nave are three equal-sized round-headed recesses, the central one framing the main door, while those to either side contained benches within a localised widening of the wall that carried a gallery. Above the gallery were three round-headed windows of equal height, and above them, filling the space below the ceiling, was a large rose window (**29**). Circular windows were a common feature of Cistercian churches, though

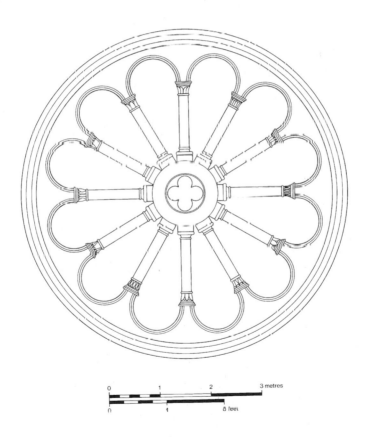

0   1   2   3 metres
0   1   8 feet

29 *Although the twelfth-century windows of the west gable were taken out at the end of the fifteenth century, substantial fragments of the original rose window have been recovered from the west gable of the church. One of the earliest Cistercian rose window to be recorded, it provides the first evidence for the softening of the order's architectural puritanism.* Stuart Harrison

30 *The galilee porch that covered the west doors of the nave was a common feature of great Cistercian churches in the twelfth and early thirteenth centuries. It was a popular burial place for lay patrons whose burial in the church was originally discouraged. It was reconstructed from fallen elements in the 1850s*

few survive today. Associated with the cult of the Virgin, they were particularly appropriate to an order whose churches were invariably dedicated to Her, though they provided an excuse for decoration that was otherwise carefully avoided. The western rose at Fountains is the second earliest known in a Cistercian context.

Externally, the west doors were covered by a porch which was a common feature of Cistercian churches. It had a central door flanked by open round-headed arcades supported on twin shafts of a design normally associated with cloister arcades (**30**). The detailing of the arcades and the west portal are comparable with the finest contemporary French Cistercian buildings.

It is possible to reconstruct the internal planning of the church from the evidence of sockets provided in the masonry to fix screens and furniture (**31**). Although the nave and transepts are now an uninterrupted space, this was not the case originally and the church was divided into a series of distinct functional compartments. This partitioning shows clearly how a major Cistercian church was used, divided between the two 'churches' of the lay brothers and choir-monks. The seven western bays of the nave comprised the lay brother's church and cuts in the seventh piers from the west indicate the position of the rood screen against which the nave altar was placed. Between the first and sixth piers of the arcade, stone walls were built against which the lay brother's stalls were ranged. The moulding of the bases is omitted where the wall was, showing that this was an original feature. The aisles were simply corridors providing access to the eastern parts of the church. Beyond the rood screen, the monks' church began. The eighth bay of the nave was their retro-choir (literally behind the choir) where the old and infirm were allowed to sit during services, in greater comfort than in the choir itself. The next bay was taken up by the pulpitum, the screen that defined the western limit of the monks' choir and which contained two chapels, that on the north dedicated to the Virgin, and that on the south to St Bernard. Over the chapels was a loft, and between them was the lower entrance to the choir. The monks' choir occupied the easternmost two bays of the nave and all of the crossing, their wooden stalls backing up against similar stone walls to those provided in the lay brothers' choir. The upper entrances to the monks' choir were immediately to the east of the eastern crossing piers, and the inner transept chapels were extended to allow the use of their western bays as vestibules. To the east, two steps defined the sanctuary within the presbytery where the main altar was placed. Nothing is known about the screening of the north transept, but it should mirror the arrangement in the south transept which is known in great detail from excavation. Here, a timber screen set in the floor closed off the transept from the crossing aisle, with an entrance at its west end, and tall parclose screens were fitted into the entrances of the middle and outer chapels. Further screens in the body of the transept enclosed spaces in front of these chapels.

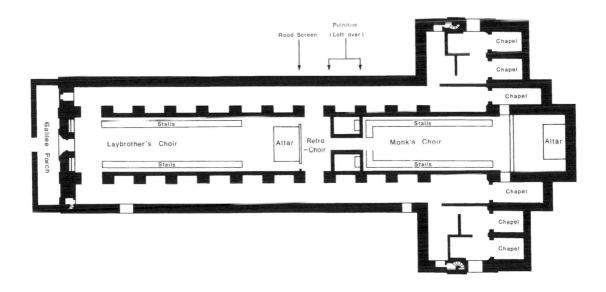

31 *The church at Fountains was divided by wooden screens into a series of discrete 'spaces', particularly the distinct churches of the choir-monks and lay brothers, and its barn-like interior was never meant to be seen as a single space.* After Peter Fergusson with additions

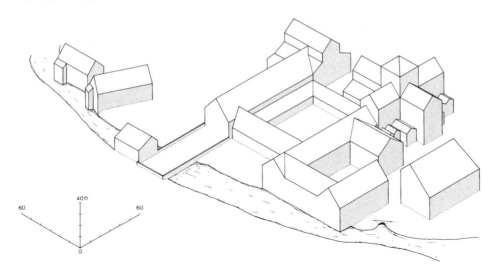

32 *A reconstruction of the church and cloister buildings as they would have appeared at the end of the abbacy of Richard of Clairvaux in 1170, with work unfinished on the church and west range*

The great church had a mortar floor throughout, except perhaps for the sanctuary which, by analogy with the contemporary church at Bordesley, might have been paved with stone flags. The only decoration was the painting of the whole building, inside and out, with limewash over which a masonry pattern was outlined in white paint. No other colour was used. The windows were glazed with plain green glass leaded in geometric or *grisaille* patterns and set in wooden frames, the fixings for which remain in the clerestory and transept chapel windows. Very few traces of the original furnishings of the church survive. For the sedile or priest's seat in the south wall of the presbytery in front of the altar, we have to look at the surviving example at Sawley. None of the original altars have been excavated, and their form is unknown. The statutes of the order forbade crosses or candlesticks of precious metal, or set with gems. Wooden altar crosses were preferred and these might be exceptionally painted. A single iron cross, perhaps from a processional staff, has survived. The church, like the cloister ranges, was roofed not in lead but with large orange ceramic tiles, which were also used to pack up undersized blocks in the structure. In all, it represents an exercise in restraint that would have compared starkly with a contemporary Benedictine or Cluniac church, a positive statement of the fundamentalism that the order espoused.

The rebuilding of the cloister

While the church was being built, the number of monks and lay brothers was steadily growing and it was not long before Murdac's cloister ranges were uncomfortably full. The only solution was to abandon work on the church in the early 1160s and concentrate instead on enlarging and rebuilding the cloister ranges (**32**). In the meantime, the lay brothers' church in the nave remained incomplete and their services must have been held elsewhere, perhaps in the monks' refectory which was not rebuilt by Abbot Richard III. Because the convent had to be housed and the constant round of services maintained during the building operations, the sequence of building became complicated in the extreme. Although this work considerably enlarged the cloister buildings, the plan adopted by Murdac was retained.

The earliest work, which almost certainly belongs to the first years of Richard's abbacy, was a new latrine block for the lay brothers (**33**), placed in the River Skell to the south and west of their original range. It was planned as a free-standing building with latrines at both ground and first-floor level (**colour plate 7**). A blocked door in the north wall at first floor level is an original feature, showing that the latrine block was entered by a wooden bridge from across the river. This indicates that the lay brothers must have been temporarily accommodated in a two-storey timber building on the north bank of the river that has yet to be excavated. Murdac's west range was then demolished to ground level with the exception of its east wall which was retained to ensure the enclosure of the cloister, and a new range was laid out that was wider, longer and higher than its predecessor. Its building proved to be a lengthy affair and the lay brothers must have occupied their temporary quarters for a decade or more.

33 *The lay brothers' latrine block, originally built as a freestanding building in the River Skell. To its east is the south end of the lay brothers' range completed by Abbot Robert of Pipewell in the 1170s*

The foundations of the range, including the four tunnels that were to carry it over the river and connect it to the latrine block, were laid out early in the 1160s and walling was carried up to just below window sill level. The new range was almost twice the size of its predecessor, 13m wide and 91.5m long, of 22 double bays. The dormitory was at first floor level. At first only the northern 13 bays were completed in the same late Norman style adopted for the church and a temporary blocking wall was built to close off the south end, allowing this part of the range to be used, most probably by the monks whose own range was the next to be rebuilt. Widening the range required alterations to be made to the new church, showing that the rebuilding was not intended when the western bays of the nave were built. In particular, a new door for day entry into the church had to be inserted to the west of the new range, and the night-stair door was moved to the west of its original location. At the south end of the completed northern half of the range a small building was provided against the west wall below the day-stair to the lay brothers' dormitory. This was the office for the cellarer whose stores were housed in the ground floor of the range between the office and the outer parlour. On the west side of the range a rectangular cloister was provided for the lay brethren, its arcade being almost identical to that of the galilee porch at the west end of the church. Instead of being supported on twin columns it had single shafts. The corbels that carried its roof can still be seen in the west wall of the range, and the plan of this new cloister has been revealed by geophysical survey.

34 *The rebuilt monks' dormitory range incorporates in its lower walling the greater part of the pre-fire range. The southern end of the range comprised the dayroom. A central row of piers originally supported a groined vault on which the dormitory floor was carried*

35 *The shattered remains of Richard of Clairvaux's chapter-house retains the bases of its marble piers and the springing and wall ribs of its vaulted ceiling. Within the railings at the east end are the graves of the abbots, starting with Richard himself and including those of Robert of Pipewell, William of Newminster, Ralph Haget, John of York, and John of Kent*

Next, attention turned to the rebuilding of the monks' accommodation in the east range where the work was less substantial but equally impressive. The southern part of the original range was retained, its windows and doors blocked up and new masonry added to raise the height of the range substantially (**34**). The groove cut in the south transept wall to take the lead flashings of the new roof can still be seen cutting across the 1150s clerestory windows. As well as raising the height of the range it was extended at its south end where a new latrine block was built on the north bank of the river, enabling the drain to be flushed directly by the Skell, an improvement on its predecessor which was too small for the growing community.

The ground floor of the range was extensively replanned. To the south of the new library and sacristy which had been intruded into the north end of the range a new chapter-house, one of the largest ever built in England, was inserted, extending well to the east like Aelred's new chapter-house at Rievaulx but of a very different plan. Aelred had adapted the Benedictine form with an apsidal east end, but at Fountains a square east end was provided. Entered from the east cloister alley by three richly moulded doors of equal height (**colour plate 8**), the room was divided into three aisles of six bays by tall, monolithic columns with foliate capitals that supported a vaulted ceiling (**35**). The two western bays within the range that served as a vestibule were vaulted at a lower level than the rest of the building to allow the dormitory floor to continue uninterrupted. The two laterals door from the cloister led not into the vestibule but into a pair of timber-screened book cupboards, providing extra library space for study in the cloister alleys. The chapter-house was second only in importance to the church for it was here that the corporate life of the community was conducted, duties allocated, faults confessed, and punishment decreed. It was also the burial-place of abbots, and Richard of Clairvaux, the first abbot to be buried at Fountains, was interred here in 1170, his grave being set centrally between the two eastern piers at the foot of the abbot's chair. His burial, in what must have been a completed building, provides a convenient date for the completion of work to the whole of the range. Unlike the church, the chapter-house was, by Cistercian standards at least, a highly-decorated building, though the two structures are broadly contemporary. Where the church is massive and Romanesque, the chapter-house is light, finely proportioned, and gothic in its inspiration. The piers that supported the vault are of grey Nidderdale marble (its first use at Fountains) that contrasted with the white paintwork of the walls and ceiling, the capitals and corbels had fine leaf decoration, and the vault had moulded ribs. A similar contrast can be seen at Rievaulx and Fontenay, and it would appear that architectural forms were adapted to function and that austerity was not necessarily all-pervading.

At the same time as the chapter-house was being built, the parlour to the south was remodelled. It had a cloister door matching the entrances to the chapter-house and a new door in the east wall leading to an enclosed yard between the new chapter-house and latrine block. It had a ribbed vault of three bays, matching that of the chapter-house, supported on triple corbels with unusual and severely beautiful leaf designs.

The southern half of the range was vaulted in seven double bays from a central row of piers (**34**). The northern bay was partitioned off by a stone wall, removed in the nineteenth century, to provide a through passage from the cloister to the infirmary that lay to the east. The first two piers from the north are complete, their capitals level with the corbels inserted into the walls of Murdac's range to carry a groined vault. Noticeably, their bases differ from the other piers. This is because they are not bases at all but reused capitals that have been inverted and which probably came from Murdac's chapter-house. The south end of the range remained the day room, still unheated. The day-stair to the dormitory was removed from its northern end, to be replaced by a stair inserted into the east end of the otherwise untouched south range, a location generally adopted by the order in the third quarter of the twelfth century.

The dormitory itself was almost entirely a new construction, its floor only slightly below the wall-head of Murdac's range. Measuring 54.3m (178ft) long and with a further 17m (55ft) above the projecting part of the chapter-house, it provided sufficient space for 120 monks, their beds placed along the walls and the central part of the room taken up by wooden clothes presses. The main body of the dormitory was lit by alternating tall, round-headed windows and small square-headed lights, while the upper storey of the chapter-house had simply round-headed windows. The raised height of the dormitory floor made the original night stair to the dormitory unusable, and a new round-headed door was pierced in the south transept wall at the height of the new floor, reached by a timber stair in the transept itself. At the head of the night stair was a vaulted chamber entered by a wide arch. This was probably the treasury or strong-room in the charge of the sacrist whose bed was placed at the transept end of the dormitory.

The ground floor of the latrine block comprised the novices' day-room in many Cistercian houses, and although at Fountains it is now reduced to low walling its original layout is still apparent. It was originally barrel-vaulted and ran the full length of the building. At its east end was an adjoining building that incorporated the east end of the monks' old latrine block and which was aligned north to south, parallel with the dormitory range (**colour plate 12**). This building, much altered in later years, was the abbot's house, its principal rooms at first-floor level with the hall to the north and bed-chamber to the south so that the abbot could maintain a link with the dormitory as he was required to do by the order's statutes. Being built in the late 1160s, it conveniently dates the period at which Cistercian abbots were moving into discrete lodgings.

Enclosed by the east range, the chapter-house, the abbot's house, and latrine was a rectangular yard with a covered alley on its west and possibly other sides, perhaps forming as at Rievaulx, a lesser cloister. At Rievaulx this second cloister was associated with the infirmary where the older members of the community and those who were sick lived a less rigorous life, but at Fountains the early infirmary lies to the north-east of the abbot's house. Only its south wall has been seen in excavation close to its south-west corner, and the line of its north and west walls can be traced from settlement cracks in buildings that now lie over them. Its date of building is unknown, but as it was taken down to extend the church in the second quarter of the thirteenth century it is likely to date from Richard of Clairvaux's time or immediately afterwards. In plan it is likely to resemble the infirmary built at Rievaulx by Abbot Aelred, with a single aisle on its east side. In scale it is much smaller, almost the same size as the early infirmary at Kirkstall. As architectural ideas seem to have been developed in the family of monasteries, it is not surprising that there should be two similar early infirmaries within the Fountains *familia*.

The earliest statutes of the order required provision to be made within Cistercian monasteries for hospitality for guests, and Abbot Richard built two guest-houses in the inner court for the most important visitors to the monastery (**36**). Each building contained a separate suite of buildings on two floors: a hall with a wall-fireplace, a chamber, and a latrine which discharged

36 *The east and west guest-houses built in the 1160s for important visitors to the abbey remain largely as they were built and are among the best surviving examples of twelfth-century domestic architecture in England. To their east is Robert of Pipewell's lay brothers' infirmary, and beyond, across the river, is the abbey's wool house*

into the river. The ground-floor suites were vaulted and of inferior quality to those on the upper floor, while the western guest-house is smaller than its eastern counterpart (**colour plate 11**). Thus accommodation of four different qualities was provided by these two buildings from the 1160s.

The 'sumptuous buildings' of Abbot Robert of Pipewell

Abbot Robert, previously Abbot of Pipewell in Northamptonshire, was elected in 1170, the first of a series of extremely competent abbots who had trained in lesser monasteries of the Fountains family. To him fell the completion of the rebuilding of the cloister ranges, the church, and the guest accommodation. Hugh of Kirkstall records in the *Narratio* that he was a capable administrator that ruled well and who provided his community with 'sumptuous buildings'.

Abbot Pipewell's first work appears to have been the completion of the nave of the church to its original plan and apart from Hugh of Kirkstall's blunt statement to that effect in the *Narratio* there is no other evidence to suggest that it had not been completed before his election. However, he also seems to have done some work to the crossing tower, for architectural detail which can only have come from the wall galleries of the lantern have been identified, showing that it was heavily influenced by the crossing towers of Byland Abbey and Ripon Minster, both of which were built early in Robert's abbacy.

He next turned his attention to the completion of the lay brothers' accommodation. The new work can be identified by the use of gothic lancet windows to light the lay brothers' refectory on the ground floor, though the windows of the dormitory above continued the original design, so far as it could be seen from the inner court (**37**). It was at this point that the ground floor rooms were vaulted (**38**). Both vault and walls retain extensive traces of the 1170s paint-scheme, a formal masonry pattern similar to that used previously but with the joints picked out by double white lines over a ground coat of limewash. The dormitory on the upper floor was larger than that provided for the lay brothers at Clairvaux itself. On the ground floor, the northern two bays comprised the outer parlour, the next six were cellarage, two bays formed the entrance to the cloister and the remaining 12 bays the lay brothers' refectory, following the same general plan as Murdac's original west range. Once the west range was finished, the lay brothers' quarters were completed by the building of an infirmary to the west of their latrine block (**36**), carried across the river on four tall tunnels. Little now remains other than the north

37 *Although it was completed over two decades, the west range of the rebuilt monastery is remarkable for its uniformity of style. The ground floor of the earlier northern half of the range was concealed by the contemporary lay brothers' cloister. Visitors would not have seen that its round-headed doors and windows differed from the lancet windows that lit the later lay brothers' refectory to the south*

wall. It was an aisled hall of six bays, a development in the Early English style that was to become the hall mark of Abbot Pipewell's buildings.

Although Pipewell's work in the west range was impressive it was overshadowed by his achievement in the reconstruction of the south cloister range. With the rebuilding of Clairvaux in the early 1140s, the Benedictine planning of a refectory parallel to the south cloister alley was abandoned, allowing the kitchen to occupy the western third of the range where it was accessible from the cloister, and the warming room to be placed in the eastern third of the range. By the early 1170s, the refectory at Fountains was distinctly old-fashioned and too small for the enlarged community. At Clairvaux, the new refectory was placed at right-angles to the south cloister alley, allowing it to be lengthened. Fountains was the first Cistercian monastery in Britain to adopt this new plan and was the model for all later buildings here.

Abbot Robert's new south cloister range was purely gothic in style and demonstrates a development of his work in the west range. Here, he was building for choir-monks, and the refectory came after only the church and chapter house in its spiritual significance. Cistercian conservatism required the suppression of unnecessary ornament but the lightness of the Early English architecture enabled Pipewell to raise buildings that remain beautiful in their simplicity (**39**).

38 *The interior of the west range is now an open space throughout its length, but it was originally divided up by stone cross walls. Much of the vault is original though the southernmost bays were rebuilt after they fell in the early nineteenth century*

39 *Seen from the lay brothers' dormitory, the composition of Robert of Pipewell's south cloister range is both simple and dramatic in its architecture*

Rebuilding the south range was a complicated business because it had to be done around Murdac's buildings which remained in use as long as possible. The earliest part of the new range was the warming-house at its east end, three storeys high (**colour plate 13**). The provision of a warming-house with two great fireplaces 4.9m (16ft) wide marked a softening in Cistercian austerity first seen in England by Aelred's provision of a fireplace in the day room of his east range at Rievaulx in the 1150s. A heated room in the cloister where fires were burned from 1 November to Good Friday was a necessity in the colder climes of northern England and it remains surprising that it took so long to be adopted at Fountains. The fires needed a copious supply of wood to feed them, and a yard was provided to the south of the warming-house that contained a wood-store built against the west wall of the east range. A bridge across the Skell enabled wood to be brought from the outer court of the monastery without disturbing the peace of the cloister.

Above the warming-room and reached from the monks' day-stair which occupied the eastern bay of the range, was a dry and fire-proof room, the muniment room in which all the abbey's deeds and estate papers were kept. Its size is not surprising because Fountains had more than 3,500 title deeds to its extensive estates, and like many other religious houses safeguarded the deeds and treasure of local families. It was probably here that King John's treasury was kept in the early part of 1215, for nine days after the signing of the *Magna Carta* he ordered that all his goods and valuables stored at Fountains be sent secretly

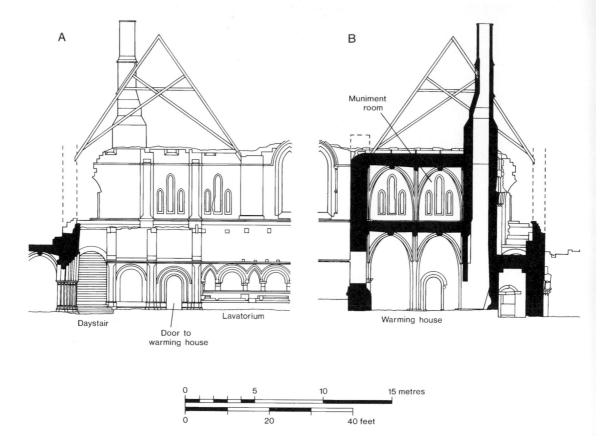

40 *A reconstruction of the roof above the warming-house and muniment room, based on the evidence of timber slots and sockets*

to him. The room was certainly secure, for not only did it have windows with iron grilles and a door closed with a draw-bar set into the masonry but there were also two further doors in the short passage that led into this room from the day-stair. Further security was ensured by placing the prior's chamber at the head of the day-stair above the wood-store where he could control access to the dormitory and the muniment room. Above the muniment room and occupying the roof-space was a further chamber, most probably used for storage but also secure, being reached by a spiral stair from the muniment room passage. The form of its roof, the only roof at Fountains for which there is clear evidence of form, can be reconstructed from the slots and sockets cut into the one surviving warming-house chimney (**40**).

Next to be built was the refectory, a remarkable building at the centre of the new south range, its door to the cloister alley flanked by deep arcades that contained the long metal basins where the monks washed their hands before meals. The pewter troughs of the *lavatorium*, removed at the suppression, were supplied with piped water and the chases for the pipes can still be identified

1 *The ruins of Fountains Abbey as they exist today.* English Heritage

2 *Like many Cistercian abbeys Fountains hides from the world in a deep valley*

HÆC SUSTENTEGONUS Q QVOD TALIA CISTE PATRONUS

HÆC HABEAT GRATVM PRESENS O HVS ACOИ GRATVS

3 (Opposite) *A contemporary illustration of Abbot Stephen Harding (right) presenting his church of Cîteaux to the Virgin; on the left is the abbot of St Vaase. Both are wearing the undyed early habit of the Cistercians.* Bibliothèque Municipale, Dijon

4 (Above) *A Cistercian monk involved in the manual labour of the harvest, from a Cîteaux manuscript, the* Moralia in Job *written during Stephen Harding's lifetime.* Bibliothèque Municipale, Dijon

5 (Below) *A Cistercian monk praying at the feet of an archangel, from the* Moralia in Job. Bibliothèque Municipale, Dijon

6 *The south transept of the second stone church at Fountains is virtually devoid of any decoration, though it is built throughout of well-cut stone*

7 *The first floor latrine seen from the lay brothers' dormitory. The upper floor latrines were on the right; the ground-floor latrines were on the left, below a wooden ceiling*

8 *The chapter-house façade survives almost intact with its three equal-height doors. Though they retain the white paint typical of Cistercian buildings, the doors have lost their black marble angle-shafts, designed to contrast with the masonry behind them*

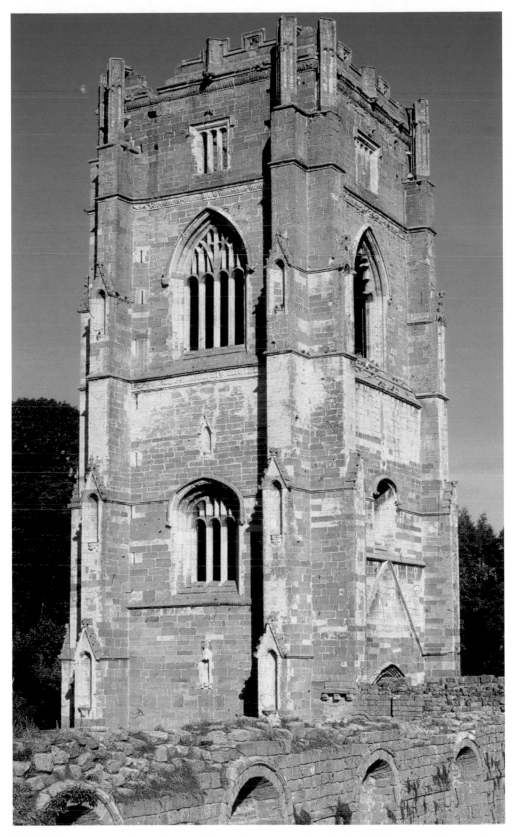

9 *Huby's new tower, attached to the end of the north transept, marks a break with Cistercian tradition, and is the finest raised by the order in the north of England*

10 *A bench-end carved by the Bromfletes of Ripon for Jervaulx Abbey in the 1520s gives a clear impression of Huby's lost choir stalls at Fountains.* Stuart Harrison

11 *The west guest-house retains good evidence of both the ground and first-floor apartments, and is one of the most complete domestic buildings to survive from the 1160s in England*

12 The basement of the abbot's house, substantially rebuilt in the late fifteenth and sixteenth centuries, with the abbot's chamber with its bay window on the left, the base of the hall fireplace in the centre, and the misericord on the extreme right

13 The south range of the cloister, with the warming-house, the eastern half of the cloister laver, and the door to the refectory

14 *An artist's reconstruction of the Chapel of Nine Altars after its remodelling and re-roofing by Abbot John Darnton in the 1480s and '90s.* Alan Sorrell/English Heritage (**colour plate 13**). Indeed, one of the bronze taps has survived, recovered by excavation in the nineteenth century (**41**). Piped water was generally introduced into monasteries from the middle of the twelfth century, and the Cistercians were in the vanguard of this development. Before the 1170s, the Cistercians had favoured the detached laver borrowed from the Benedictines and Cluniacs, a fountain with surrounding washing troughs often placed in its own house attached to the south walk of the cloister and frequently still seen in European houses of the order. At Fountains, geophysical survey suggests that the original laver house stood in the south-west corner of the cloister garth; its removal to the inner wall of the alley, commonly seen in Britain from the end of the twelfth century, seems to have begun at Fountains. Water for the laver was collected in a tank in the south-east corner of the precinct (see Chapter Five) and piped to the cloister though a series of well houses (of which the late twelfth-century Robin Hood's Well is the only survivor) and conduits. A separate supply was engineered for the lay brothers. Little is known in detail of the water supply at Fountains because it has yet to be examined by excavation, but the examination of the contemporary water-works at Kirkstall and Sawley has shown that it is likely to be very sophisticated indeed.

The refectory was conceived as a building of five double bays with a central arcade, each bay lit by a pair of tall lancet windows. Its length posed a problem because the old yard to the south of Murdac's refectory in which it was built was bounded to the south by the river, leaving insufficient space for the new building. The river could not be moved because it serviced both the lay brothers' and monks' latrines, and the only solution was to build the southernmost half-bay of the building over the river on a tunnel. Construction was from south to north, with a temporary pause against the south wall of the earlier refectory

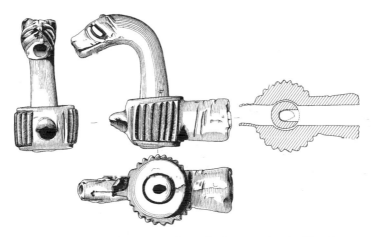

41 *A cast bronze tap from the cloister laver gives a clue to the decoration that the Cistercians were coming to accept by the last quarter of the twelfth century. Its survival in use up to the sixteenth century shows how reliable the piped water system at Fountains was*

42 *The refectory has lost the arcade down its centre which supported the double-pitched roof, and the reader's pulpit has gone, but it still retains the footpaces around its walls and the stone legs of its tables. The twelfth-century roof was replaced by one of a flatter pitch in the fifteenth century, but the gable walls still retain the bottoms of two circular windows that filled its original twin gables.* English Heritage

which remained in use as long as possible. Finally, a section of the old refectory was demolished and the rebuilding completed (**42**), the final work being carried out in stone of a slightly different colour leaving a joint which is still apparent.

Within, the new refectory was an impressive building, open to the roof and divided down its centre by an arcade. As originally built, the refectory was roofed in two spans, a feature of the contemporary refectory at Fontenay, and each span was lit by a circular window in its southern gable. The roof was altered to one of a single span and lower pitch in the fifteenth century but otherwise the refectory retains its original detailing. The walls were white-washed and lined out in white paint to resemble ashlar masonry, and although most of this has now been lost some remains in the splays of the western windows, showing that the monotony of plain block-work was relieved with geometric patterns which perhaps reflected the grisaille windows.

Raised foot-paces or platforms were provided against the east and west walls and these retain the bases of the stone legs that supported long tables for the monks, whose stone benches were placed against the side walls, three on the east and two on the west as access to the kitchen precluded a third table there. The tunnel that carried the southern half-bay of the building over the Skell provided the base for a broad dais on which the prior's table was set. Because custom required the abbot to eat with guests the prior was to preside over the

43 *The kitchen in the south range of the cloister, with the round-headed hatch into the refectory. The block of masonry in the centre is one side of the huge double fireplace that filled the centre of the room and rose through the vaulted ceiling*

convent's meals, twice a day in summer and once in winter. Meals were taken in silence, only interrupted by readings from the Bible. A round-headed door in the west wall led to a stair in the thickness of the wall that gave access to a passage and the reader's pulpit carried on a great foliate corbel that still remains.

The last part of the south range to be rebuilt was the kitchen (**43**), placed to serve both the monks' refectory and that of the lay brothers in the west range. A round-headed opening to the monks' refectory was not a door for the jambs are convex, instead the opening was originally fitted with a circular dumb-waiter revolving on a pivot. A similar, smaller opening to the lay brothers' refectory once existed but has been blocked up. At the centre of the kitchen, which prepared only vegetarian meals for meat was not allowed to healthy monks, were two great fireplaces set back-to-back with a chimney passing through the roof. As originally built, the kitchen was open to the roof, and to reduce the heat three unglazed pointed arches pieced the north wall above the cloister roof and a wide arch was provided in the south wall. This door led to a yard on the south side of the kitchen where firewood was stored. Kitchens were a notorious fire-risk and shortly after the completion of Abbot Robert's new kitchen vaulted ceilings were inserted to protect the timber roof. Though they no longer survive, clear traces can be seen of three bays of vaulting in the northern half of the building, and two to the south of the chimney.

44 *Reconstructed from fragments dumped in the east guest-house in the late eighteenth century, Robert of Pipewell's cloister arcade is the most elaborate of the Cistercian twelfth-century cloister arcades known in England. The leaf decoration on its marble capitals has been omitted in this drawing*

Following the completion of the south range, Robert of Pipewell completed the development of the central monastic buildings with the construction of a splendid new cloister arcade (**44**), linking the completed cloister buildings and church and providing the monks' living room at the heart of the monastery. Though ruthlessly swept away in the 1770s, many of its elements have been discovered and it is possible to reconstruct it with a high degree of accuracy. Twin shafts of black Nidderdale marble with matching capitals and bases supported trefoil arches of sandstone which were whitelimed to provide contrast. Porches projected into the cloister garth at the centre of the north and south alleys. That on the north contained the abbot's seat where he heard Collation, that on the south had a door that matched that of the refectory and provided access to the cloister garth itself where there was probably a garden. Although the arcades were not glazed, the cloister alleys at Fountains were the finest constructed by the Cistercians in England, and if they lacked the simplicity that St Bernard sought, they amply demonstrated the status of the abbey as the mother house of an important family.

The final building which can be associated with Abbot Robert was a new guest hall (**45**), built on the north side of the two earlier guest-houses and

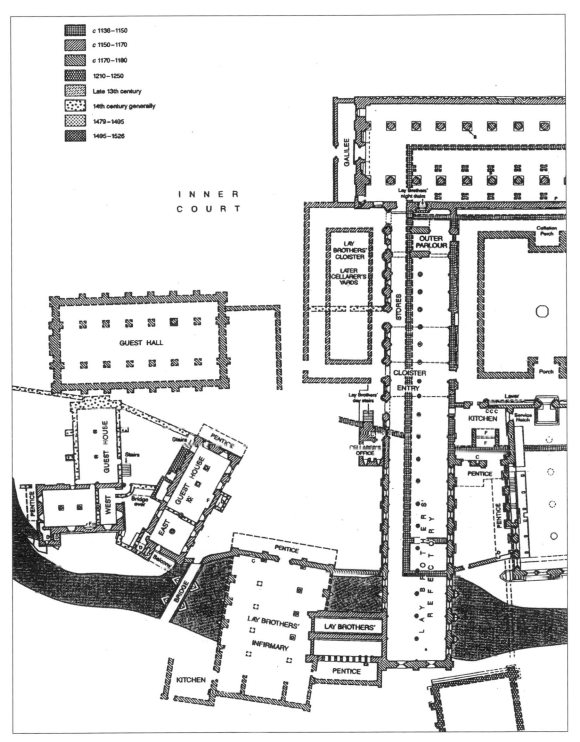

45 *Known only from geophysical survey and a single surviving pier base, the new guest-hall, seen in this section of the survey, completed the development of guest facilities at Fountains. Sections of its quatrefoil piers can be seen in the floor of the woolhouse, indicating that the building was probably taken down in the early fifteenth century*

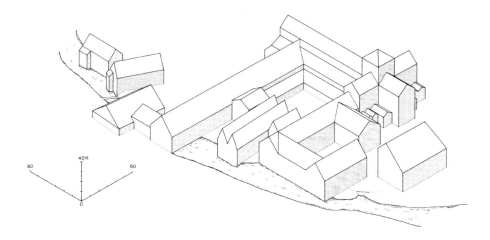

46 *On the death of Abbot Pipewell, the rebuilt monastery was complete, its buildings comparing well with any other great Cistercian monastery in Europe and providing a convincing illustration of the scale and disposition of the central buildings of the head of a family*

providing accommodation for less important guests. The *Narratio* notes that Pipewell was remembered for his hospitality to rich and poor alike. Only small fragments of this building are visible today but its plan has been recovered by geophysical survey, an aisled hall of seven bays, its buttresses suggesting that the aisles were vaulted, with a large fireplace at the centre of its west wall. All that remains today is the late twelfth century base of one of its northern arcade piers and the stump of a table leg next to the pier. The remainder of the table leg is still lying where it fell when the building was demolished. Tables were placed between the piers of the arcades.

The death of Abbot Robert in 1180 marks the completion of the second major stage in the life of the abbey (**46**). The community had been provided with a great church and fine cloister buildings that reflected the house's importance within the order, it had expanded to its optimum size, and it had achieved sufficient wealth to support itself and indulge in monumental building works. Now was the time for a period of consolidation, with abbots more noted for their spirituality than their administrative genius. The purpose of the community, after all, was to praise God through prayer, meditation, and manual labour, and great building works must have been a dreadful distraction.

4

THE SOFTENING OF CISTERCIAN IDEALS

The election of William of Newminster as abbot in 1180 marks the start of a period of consolidation. An old man, wasted by continual austerity, he had been professed at Augustinian Guisborough but had joined the Cistercians at Fountains' first daughter house of Newminster and in time became the abbot there. He was not a builder but a wise and vigorous administrator who ruled with gentleness. Dying in 1190, he was succeeded by Ralph Haget, an ex-soldier who had entered Fountains on the advice of his friend Sinnulph, a lay brother of the house. For nine years he had been abbot of the daughter house of Kirkstall where he had proved to be of no great administrative ability. His greatest qualities were his spirituality, wit and charm. In him the community found a leader they could love and respect. He died in 1203 and his death marks the beginning of the next phase in the abbey's development. It also marked a change in the order, for from the beginning of the thirteenth century the Cistercians began to loose many of the characteristics that had set them apart from unreformed Benedictines. In particular, this softening of ideals is demonstrated in the new buildings raised at Fountains in the first half of the thirteenth century.

The rebuilding of the abbey church

By 1180, after less than half a century, the buildings of Fountains Abbey had achieved a greater scale than any other house of the order in England, including the great neighbouring abbey of Rievaulx. Between 1203 and 1247 the abbey was to see even more extensive building as the Cistercians became wealthier and more willing to accept a lessening degree of architectural puritanism. Richard of Clairvaux's choir and presbytery of the 1150s was no longer fashionable, long overshadowed by the great aisled presbytery of Byland built in the early 1170s, and the community complained that it was cramped and dark. It was decided to replace the old two-bay presbytery with a great aisled eastern arm of five bays. The building of this occupied the abbacies of three Johns: John of York, John of Hessle, and John of Kent.

John of York, who became abbot on Haget's death, had a similar career to his predecessor. In turn he had been a monk, then cellarer of Fountains, and then abbot of the daughter house of Louth Park before he returned to the

47 *The new presbytery was a light and gothic structure which contrasted strongly with the earlier nave. Though the arcades and clerestory have fallen enough fragments have been recovered to reconstruct them.* English Heritage

mother house. To him belongs the decision to rebuild the eastern parts of the church. The model he chose to follow was the four-bay aisled presbytery of Jervaulx Abbey that had only recently been completed. Jervaulx appears to have been the first Cistercian church in England to have adopted a form of aisled choir-arm with a stark, square east wall already used by the Benedictines at Whitby and Tynemouth and the Augustinians at Hexham. Although the church at Jervaulx has been destroyed to the level of its plinth, large numbers of its architectural elements can still be identified on site and the technical similarities that these pieces display to the surviving structure at Fountains would suggest that the same master mason was involved. The height of the existing transepts and nave, which were to be retained, required that the new work should match the two-storey elevation of Richard of Clairvaux's church, but in architectural terms it was a very different building. Gone were the heavy cylindrical piers of the nave, round-headed windows, and wooden ceiling of the main span. In their place was a light and very gothic structure with tall lancet windows, a wealth of moulded detail, and a vaulted ceiling over the main span as well as the aisles (**47**). Only the outer walls of this new presbytery survive, for the arcades had fallen and been cleared away by the third quarter of the eighteenth century. Enough remains to reconstruct its elevation with a high degree of certainty (**48**).

The new aisles opened out of the inner mid-twelfth-century transept chapels and were divided from the main body of the presbytery by alternating piers of octagonal and clustered form. The clustered piers were of black Nidderdale marble. Along the outer walls of the aisles was an arcade with trefoiled heads carried on Nidderdale marble shafts above a wall bench, and this arcade matched a free-standing arcade inside the main vessel of the presbytery that enclosed the altar and the area in front of it. The aisles were lit by tall lancet windows with grisaille glass in wooden frames, the fixings for which still survive, flanked by rather curious and probably experimental arcading that follows the profile of the vault. Fallen detail from the upper part of the presbytery shows that its clerestory matched the slightly later work that survives to the east. The traditional upper storeys of triforium and clerestory were combined, each bay with a single lancet window flanked by blind arcades fronted by a wall-passage and gallery framed by the wall ribs of the high vault. The walls were covered with a buff limewash on which a masonry pattern was painted in white, contrasting with all the black marble shafts that emphasised the height of the building.

John of York must have begun the project late in his abbacy, for at his death in 1211 the *Narratio* records that he only completed a few of the piers.

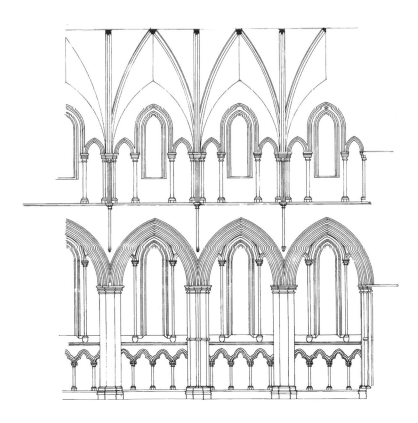

48 *Reconstructed from fallen elements, three bays on the north side of the early thirteenth-century presbytery show that it was a sophisticated composition which contrasted starkly with the earlier nave and transepts.*
Stuart Harrison

Presumably he was building around the earlier church and the old presbytery would only be demolished when the new choir arm was reaching completion. His successor, John of Hessle, who left Fountains in 1220 to become Bishop of Ely, must have continued the work and brought the new building of five bays into the church. In spite of the monks' complaints about their old choir it remained in the nave and crossing until the suppression. Rievaulx was to follow Fountains' lead, beginning the construction of an aisled choir arm of seven bays in the second decade of the thirteenth century that was conceived from the first as a much grander and expensive building of three full storeys (**49**). It brought Rievaulx close to bankruptcy and caused Fountains to think bigger.

The buildings of Abbot John of Kent

John of Kent's greatest contribution was the addition of an eastern transept, the Chapel of Nine Altars, to the east of the new presbytery. This remarkable building remains virtually intact apart from its roof and vaults. It has no Cistercian model (**50**), indeed the only comparable building is the eastern transept of the Benedictine cathedral priory of Durham begun in 1242 as a copy of the Fountains building. It effectively added two bays in length to the presbytery and was nine narrow bays in length. It was built to provide a series of nine chapels against the east wall of the church, needed by the growing numbers of monks who were also priests and required to say a personal Mass. The fact that Clairvaux had nine chapels around its eastern apse is significant, for Fountains, rather than Rievaulx that had the better claim, was projecting itself as the 'English Clairvaux' (**51**).

Architecturally, the Chapel of Nine Altars continued the design of the presbytery, though its detailing shows a degree of development. Each bay had a lancet window flanked by blind arcading set over a continuous wall arcade that matched that of the presbytery aisles, with a similar arrangement in the clerestory fronted by a wall-passage and gallery. In the eastern gable of the church, in place of the three central lancets of the clerestory, was a great rose window, removed in 1483 by Abbot Darnton, that balanced Richard of Clairvaux's circular window in the west gable of the nave. Many elements of this window have been recovered (**52**) showing that it was an elaborate feature, a contrasting combination of black marble spokes and white-painted sandstone rings within a heavily moulded rim picked out with red and black paint. The inner face of the rose window was rebated to take glazed panels in wooden frames which must have been fitted in position as the window was built and acted as centring. The design of the circular window was picked up in the elaborate mosaic tile floors that John of Kent laid in the presbytery and Nine Altars after 1236, fragments of which can still be seen reset in the platform of the high altar. Their loss is unfortunate

49 *Rievaulx's three-storey presbytery, modelled on Benedictine Whitby, was built to rival the new presbytery at Fountains, and was almost certainly the cause of building the Nine Altars.* English Heritage

50 *The eastern transept of the Nine Altars was designed to impress, though it could only be seen across the convent cemetery and was almost invisible from outside the precinct.* English Heritage

51 *The Chapel of Nine Altars, modified in the late fifteenth century when its high vaults were taken down and new windows inserted, continued the architectural design of the presbytery to which it was added in the second quarter of the thirteenth century.* English Heritage for they were probably the first mosaic tile floors to be laid in northern England. Only Beaulieu Abbey in Hampshire has earlier tiles, dated to the completion of the presbytery there in about 1227. The form of the Fountains pavements must have been similar to those that still survive at Byland, with elaborate roundels in front of the altars and great areas of 'carpet' defining the most important areas.

Although the inspiration for the new presbytery was entirely English – indeed the same master was responsible for the eastern arm of Beverley Minster where identical detailing can still be seen – there remained a strong element of Cistercian restraint apparent in the architecture. Dog-tooth decoration, much loved by both the Benedictines and Augustinians, was noticeably absent, only occurring on the rim of the eastern rose window, and the key stones of the high and aisle vaults were not decorated with carved bosses but were simply distinguished by being carved in black marble to contrast with the painted sandstone of the web of ribs that decorated and supported the vault.

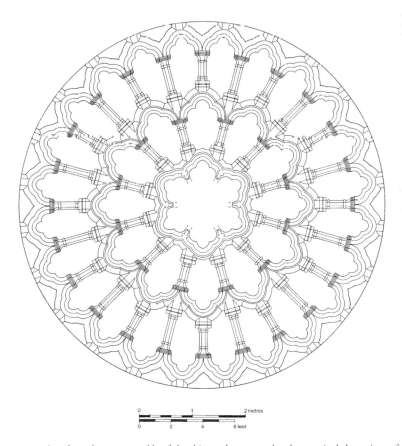

52 *The rose window from the eastern gable of the thirteenth-century church comprised three rings of trefoiled lights. No parts of the outer ring have yet been recovered and it is assumed it followed the same form as the inner ring. The whole window was enclosed within a moulded rim with dog-tooth decoration, painted in white, red and black.* Stuart Harrison

53 *John of Kent's new infirmary was built on tunnels over the river, and though it is now ruined to the level of its plinths, enough detail survives to reconstruct its original form, one of the largest aisled halls ever built in medieval England*

Although more elaborate than the mid-twelfth-century scheme that survived in the nave and transepts, there was a studied formality to the decoration of the presbytery and Nine Altars which was peculiarly Cistercian.

John of Kent's extension of the presbytery to build the Nine Altars was achievable only at a cost. While most of the new building lay in the convent cemetery and required the moving of graves that would otherwise be disturbed, the south-eastern corner of the new transept required the demolition of the infirmary that occupied part of the site. As a consequence he was obliged to build a new infirmary and one that was to accord with the size and status of his monastery. It had to lie south of the church so that it was accessible from the cloister but there was insufficient space to the north of the river on which to build, and the land rose too steeply on the south bank of the Skell, preventing building there. Four great tunnels, some 75m (254ft) long, were constructed across the river in a remarkable feat of engineering to provide a platform on which the new infirmary could be built (**53**). Little remains of his infirmary apart from low walling and foundations, but its excavation in the mid-nineteenth century recovered many fragments of its superstructure.

This infirmary was one of the largest aisled halls ever built in medieval England. It comprised a hall of eight bays, flanked by aisles which were carried rounds the ends of the building. Fireplaces were situated centrally in its north and south walls, and beds were ranged along the side walls in the aisles. Each bay of the aisle had a single window of two lights with a circular light in the plate tracery of the head, rebated for shutters or more probably to hold glass in wooden frames (**54**). The arcades were supported on elegant circular piers with bandings and four detached shafts of Nidderdale marble. The fallen springers of the arcade that remain on site, plain towards the aisles but finely moulded towards the nave, indicate that the aisles were not vaulted but had open timber roofs. The nave had no clerestory but the whole building was covered with a single roof. Perhaps more than any other building at Fountains, the grand new infirmary, itself a separate monastery for the old and infirm members of the community, indicates the wealth and status that Fountains had achieved by the second quarter of the thirteenth century.

Abbot John also provided other buildings within the infirmary complex (**62**), for his tunnels provided a platform for building to the east and west of the infirmary hall. Only one of these has survived later rebuilding, a two-storey block to the east of the hall and separated from it by a small yard. Its original use is not certain. To the west of the infirmary and above the two northern tunnels is a much altered building which in its original form was the infirmary latrine block. Seven latrine shafts on the line of the south wall discharge into the river below, and as they are contemporary with the construction of the tunnels themselves this building must be part of John of Kent's original work.

Connecting the infirmary to the cloister ranges was a gallery (**55**), which can be identified with John of Kent's documented new infirmary cloister, its walls pierced with open arcades. The eastern half of the gallery with a passage to the north connecting with the south end of the Chapel of Nine Altars was built first, lit by groups of three trefoil-headed unglazed openings supported on twin shafts in both walls. Between the openings were short lengths of walling with blind arcading, strengthened by shallow, external buttresses. John of Kent's infirmary cloister must have been an exquisite structure. Either John, or less likely his successor, Stephen of Eston, completed the gallery to the west, where the architectural detail was slightly more developed.

Apart from two remarkable buildings in the outer court, very little remains of Abbot John's other buildings. His recorded work in the guest-house complex is largely unknown but must have been substantial. Of his almonry nothing is known at all, not even its site, though it must lie on the west side of the inner court to the west of the guest-houses. One further major structure, the precinct wall (**56**), appears to date from John's abbacy though it might have been begun in that of John of Hessle, for it contains reused architectural material that can only have come from the east end of the mid-twelfth-century church. This wall, 3.4m high to the top of its coping, enclosed the abbey on its west, south, and east sides, defining a precinct of some 28.3ha. The north side was closed by the quarried cliff-face that still marks the

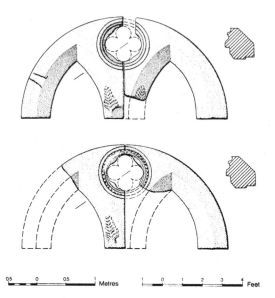

54 *Two of the window-heads recovered from the infirmary by excavation in the 1850s and which give a good indication of the quality of the building.* Simon Hayfield

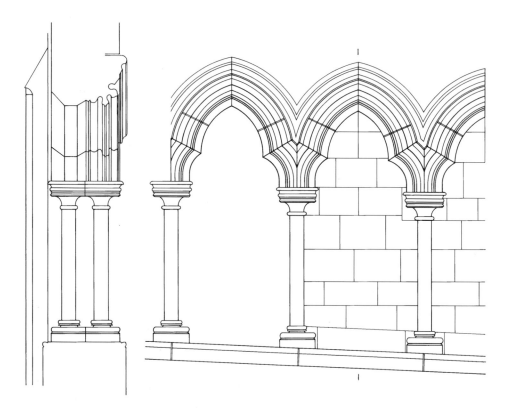

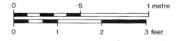

55 *Many architectural elements survive from John of Kent's infirmary gallery or cloister which have enabled its reconstruction.* Stuart Harrison

56 *The enclosing precinct wall stands to full height on both the west and south sides of the abbey*

northern edge of the Skell valley. Somewhat smaller than the 37.2ha of the enclosed precinct at Rievaulx, it was still a substantial area to enclose. The average extent of a monastic precinct in England was roughly 10ha.

On John's death in 1247, Fountains had experienced four major building campaigns in 115 years and the community must have longed for a succession of abbots who did not wish to make their mark as builders. In this they were fortunate, for on the completion of John's schemes the abbey was to see no major building work until the second half of the fifteenth century. In any case, the buildings of Fountains Abbey in 1250 would have stood favourable comparison with any other major monastery in Europe (**57**).

Fountains in the late thirteenth and fourteenth century

On John of Kent's death, Fountains was at the height of its wealth and prestige. Twelfth-century land grants and sound estate management, coupled with the exploitation of an army of lay brothers, had made the abbey the richest of its order in England. Much of the wealth was derived from sheep, though the abbey had developed a mixed economy. Although the annual wool-clip provided sufficient to meet the running costs of the house and had funded the building work of the late twelfth and thirteenth centuries it was subject to the vagaries of the market-place. Wool brought ready money but it could also bring disaster. It was sold to the great continental firms of wool-merchants, sometimes several years in advance against a substantial payment, providing a ready temptation for the convent to anticipate its real revenue. If the clip fell short of the contract, the house was obliged to buy in the deficit at a higher price. This happened to Fountains in the second half of the thirteenth century, bringing the house to the verge of bankruptcy. By 1274 the abbey was £900 in debt to the Jews of York because of wool speculation, and although the king

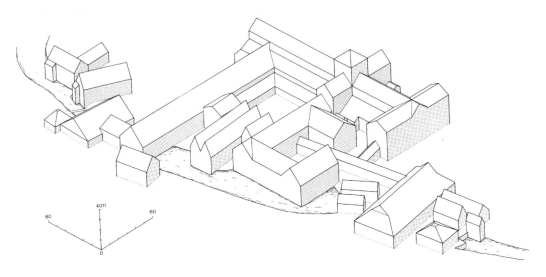

57 *The central buildings of the abbey had reached their greatest extent by 1250 when Fountains was at the height of its power and influence and were to remain in this form until the last years of the fifteenth century*

installed a lay commissioner, Peter Willoughby, to sort out the abbey's finances, renewed speculation by Abbots Peter Ayling (who pledged the abbey itself as security for a four-year contract to supply wool to Florentine merchants), Henry Otley and Robert Thornton left the abbey in debt to the tune of £6373. Then, the king was forced to impose his justiciar John of Berwick on the convent to achieve some measure of financial stability. The founding community would have been appalled, not only by such dreadful mismanagement but also by the willingness of the monks to involve themselves with money. Gone was the poverty and simplicity of life they had sought.

For all its problems the abbey was still a major power in the land. It settled down to a period of reasonable stability, reflected more in its buildings than the spirituality of its monks. Throughout the late thirteenth and fourteenth centuries no major buildings were raised and any work that was undertaken was in the area of the infirmary, abbot's house, the guest-houses and the buildings of the outer court, largely indicative of the changes in monastic life and economy seen elsewhere at this period.

The alteration of the church to suit a changing way of life

The period 1264 to 1436 was one of crisis and controversy for Fountains, with domestic mismanagement and national crisis overshadowing religious life. For ten years after the defeat of the English army at Bannockburn in 1314, the north was destabilised by Scottish raids, and the abbey itself was occupied by a large part of the Scots army in 1318. Abbot Walter Coxwold, hard pressed to maintain his convent, was required to raise men for the king to fight the Scots in 1318 and 1321, and in 1322 against the abortive rebellion of the earl of Lancaster. The spirit of lawlessness pervading the north continued until the middle years of the fourteenth century and had a dramatic effect on the economic and religious life of the abbey. With many of its estates bordering on ruin, Fountains could no longer rely on a steady supply of recruits for its army of lay brothers and by the middle of the fourteenth century they had virtually ceased to exist as a separate class within the monastery. The number of monks also declined as income fell, and in 1380/1 only 34 monks and 10 lay brothers are recorded in the abbey. At the same time, Rievaulx only had 15 monks and three lay brothers.

The ruined shell of the abbey church shows little indication that it had been altered since the completion of the Chapel of Nine Altars, so thoroughly has it been stripped of its fittings. However, major changes did take place from the early fourteenth century which can be reconstructed from the little evidence that does survive. The removal of the lay brothers' choir from the nave permitted a major replanning of the church, displaying a development of the Cistercian liturgy (**58**). Precisely when this happened is uncertain but the new layout predated the burial of Abbot John Ripon in 1434/5. We know that Fountains' daughter-house of Meaux underwent a similar replanning in the 1390s and it is unlikely that the mother-house would not have reorganised its church before then.

The reduced number of monks in the late fourteenth century was reflected by a reduction in the size of the choir which was shortened by a bay at its west end and a new pulpitum screen was provided between the first pair of piers to the west of the crossing. The bay of the nave thus emptied was provided with a great loft at the height of the old pulpitum screen that remained between the second pair of piers. On this loft, which extended into the north aisle, was an organ, for which the fixings of the case remain in the spandrels of the north arcade. Meaux had two organs in 1396, the 'great organ at the west end of the nave and a lesser organ in the choir', and it is quite possible that the same provision was made at Fountains in the later fourteenth century. Below the loft, parclose screens were placed between the nave piers, to enclose the lower entry to the choir. West of the old pulpitum, the chapels of St Mary and St Bernard were retained and the retrochoir in the fourth bay was provided with benches between the piers of the arcades. Because the aisles no longer functioned as through-passages, they could be partitioned off to form individual chapels, five in the south aisle and four in the north, their altars set against the west face of the arcade piers where the tiled platforms can still be seen. Such chapels are a common feature of Cistercian churches, and can still be seen at Byland and Roche, and were provided at Rievaulx from the last years of the thirteenth century (**59**). Little

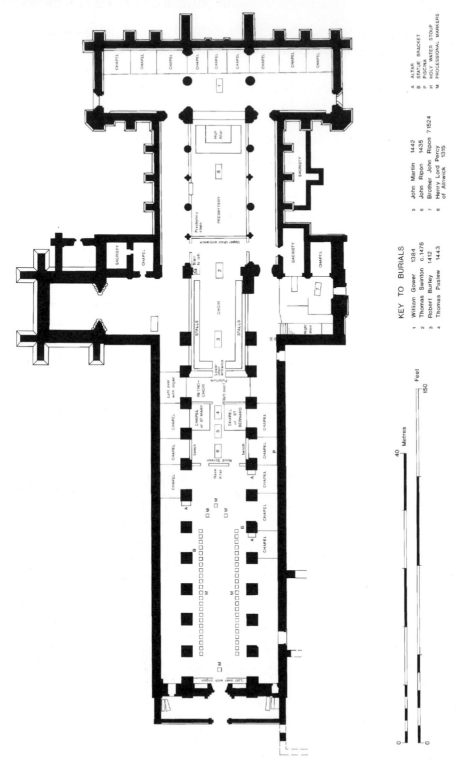

KEY TO BURIALS

1 William Gower   1384
2 Thomas Swinton   c.1478
3 Robert Burley   1412
4 Thomas Paslew   1443
5 John Martin   1442
6 John Ripon   1435
7 Brother John Ripon ?1524
8 Henry Lord Percy   1315
   of Alnwick

A ALTAR
B STATUE BRACKET
P PISCINA
H HOLY WATER STOUP
M PROCESSIONAL MARKERS

58 *The later medieval planning of the church can be determined from the marks left by its wooden screens on the masonry, the evidence of excavation and documents. This plan shows the features of the fourteenth- to sixteenth-century church and should be compared with* **31**

trace now remains of these chapels at Fountains, for their timber parclose screens have left only the evidence of their fixings in the masonry. At Rievaulx, a list of their furnishings has survived, showing that their altars were substantially dressed, and it is possible that four fragments derived from two retables depicting the four Evangelists were part of the furnishings of these new side chapels (**60**).

A second major change was the permitting of burials within the church, first of major patrons and later of abbots. Patronal burials had long been allowed in the cemetery and cloister, and such a group is known outside the chapter-house. The northernmost burial of this group, which lay outside the entrance to the library, was found on excavation to date to the late twelfth century. This group of burials is likely to include William de Percy II who died in about 1174. By the early thirteenth century, burials were being placed in the galilee porch at the west end of the church, two perhaps being the burials of William de Stuteville and Matilda Countess of Warwick who both died in 1203. The convent must have been coming under increasing pressure to permit burials within the church itself as other orders allowed. At Bordesley Abbey, the only Cistercian house to have provided detailed information, excavation has shown that burial began in the church in the late thirteenth century. Judging from surviving grave effigies at Cistercian houses such as Furness, Dore, Deer, Dundrennan, Hailes, Jervaulx, Kirkstead, Margam, Neath, Rievaulx, and Strata Florida, patronal burials began within the church in the last quarter of the thirteenth century.

59 *One of the chapels on the north side of the nave at Rievaulx, contemporary with the nave chapels at Fountains but retaining the remains of its altar, paving, and screens*

60 *Part of a fourteenth-century retable, one of two by the same carver found at Fountains, depicting St Luke, author of the third Gospel, shown seated with a pen and scroll. It probably comes from one of the nave chapels but its findspot is not recorded.* English Heritage

The first recorded burial in the presbytery at Fountains was Roger, Lord Mowbray, in 1298. The site of his burial is not known but a coffin between the second and third piers of the north arcade marks a patronal burial and others probably occupy the spaces between the other piers lining the open space before the high altar, their superstructures replacing the trefoil-headed arcade that had enclosed the altar space. What had been reserved as a liturgical area was now given over as a mausoleum for the great northern families whose ancestors had endowed the abbey. In 1315, Henry Percy, Lord of Alnwick, was buried in the centre of the presbytery before the high altar itself, and his tomb cover has survived (**61**), a military figure in a hauberk of chain-mail. Fountains was no longer just the workplace of the 'New Soldiers of Christ', it was now the burial place of the old military order.

Where the laity began, abbots were soon to follow. As the chapter-house filled up, they turned their eyes to the church. The first abbot to be buried there, behind the high altar at the centre of the Nine Altars, was William Gower who died in 1384. The next president-burial was that of Robert Burley in 1410 at the centre of the choir. A fragment of his Nidderdale marble tomb slab now lies in the northern chapel of the south transept. He was followed in 1435 by Abbot John Ripon whose grave was placed in the retrochoir. The next abbot, John Martin, was buried to the east of Ripon in 1442, and his successor Thomas Paslew was buried the following year at the entrance to the choir. Finally, Thomas Swinton was buried after 1478 between the monks' choir and the presbytery step, his gravestone with the indent of a now-missing brass still visible in the turf (**62**).

61 *The tomb-effigy of Henry Percy of Alnwick, showing a knight wearing a voluminous hauberk of chain mail beneath a sleeveless surcoat, is a product of the Cheyne workshop in York. Traces of paint survive.* Simon Hayfield

62 *The ledger slab of Abbot Thomas Swinton's grave survives between the eastern crossing piers. Although the brass insets have been plundered and the stone was broken during excavation in 1840, the outline of the abbot's figure with a mitre above his head and below a canopy can still be observed. The placing of the mitre above his head is a reference to Swinton's resignation in 1478.* Simon Hayfield

Further modification of the church in the late fifteenth and early sixteenth centuries

By the second half of the fifteenth century, the structure of the church was beginning to show its age and there is evidence to suggest that both the crossing and the eastern arm were failing structurally. Abbot Greenwell had improved the interior of the church, laying new tile pavements in the nave and transepts (**63**), and providing a stone night-stair from the church to the dormitory, but he did nothing to repair or modernise the building itself. It fell to two of the greatest abbots of the house, John Darnton and Marmaduke Huby, to restore the church to a state fitting the greatest and richest house of the Cistercian order in England.

Abbot Darnton inherited a church which was distinctly old-fashioned and showing signs of instability. Stresses from the crossing tower and presbytery had caused the south-east crossing pier to deform and a huge buttress was built to support it. Poor maintenance and over-ambitious building was starting to take its toll. Darnton found that the high vaults of the presbytery and Chapel of Nine Altars were in a dangerous state. The south-east corner of the Nine Altars, which had settled differentially over the footings of the first infirmary, was so unstable that it required shoring up. His reaction was to remodel the eastern parts of the church, removing the vaults of the main vessels, cutting back their springers, and replacing them with a new open timber roof (**colour plate 10**). Where the masonry had faulted over windows he inserted stitches of new masonry. A gap in the head of the northern window of the east wall of the Nine Altars was patched with a stone carved with a 'green man's' head and an angel carrying a scroll with the date 1483, while the head of the east window of the south wall was repaired with a figure of St James of Compostela supported on the head of an abbot, probably a portrait of Darnton himself (**64**). He went on to modernise the Chapel of Nine Altars with the insertion of new windows in the north and south gables and a vast east window of nine lights that occupied the three central bays of the chapel and removed all the original fenestration and intervening wall there. Externally, great buttresses were built to support the central part of the Nine Altars. Below the great new window, the three central chapels were united as a single chapel. Examination of the thirteenth-century windows of the presbytery and Nine Altars shows that the original glazing in wooden frames was removed at this time and replaced by new glass set into the masonry. Only fragments of the borders now survive but loose fragments of glass show that the new glazing was pictorial rather than geometric.

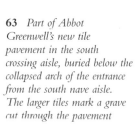

63 *Part of Abbot Greenwell's new tile pavement in the south crossing aisle, buried below the collapsed arch of the entrance from the south nave aisle. The larger tiles mark a grave cut through the pavement*

64 *A repair by John Darnton of a dislocated window-head in the south wall of the Nine Altars was carved with a portrait of Darnton himself wearing a mitre and supporting two dolphins and a scroll below a figure of St James of Compostela, identified by the cockle shell on his satchel. The scroll was probably painted with Darnton's motto Benedicite Fontes Domino.* Judith Dobie

65 *One of the new windows provided by John Darnton lights an extension to the inner chapel of the south transept that he converted into a new sacristy. Identical windows were inserted into the nave aisles.* English Heritage

Once the repair of the eastern arm was complete, John Darnton turned his attention to the transepts and nave which he reroofed at the lower pitch he had established for the presbytery. The reduction in pitch suggests that it was only then that the roofs were covered with lead, and a reduction in the pitch of the refectory roof would suggest that this improvement was not simply restricted to the church.

The twelfth century nave was distinctly old-fashioned but little used except for the chapels in the aisles. However, Darnton replaced all but two of the aisle windows with more modern traceried lights (**65**). The windows he left unaltered were those that lit the choir entrance below the loft of the pulpitum and which were barely visible inside the building. He also provided a new west window to balance the east window of the presbytery, completing the work in the year before his death. Above the window in the west wall of the church is a niche containing a statue of the Virgin and Child supported on a bracket carved with an eagle (the symbol of St John) and a barrel or tun with the letters DERN and the date 1494 on a scroll. This carving, a *rebus*, puns on the name John Darnton and is effectively his signature on the completion of his works. Of Darnton's internal decoration of the church there is little evidence. He redecorated the eastern arm by overpainting the original masonry patterning with plain limewash, but he must also have refitted the chapels of the Nine Altars and nave that he altered, replacing their stone dividing walls with timber parcloses. Perhaps it was from one of these that three alabaster retable panels found in the nineteenth century come (**66**).

Although John Darnton had modernised the structure of the church, his work is overshadowed by that of his successor, Marmaduke Huby. Abbot Huby was a great builder, made more significant than his predecessor because his principal contribution to the abbey survives virtually intact. In common with most Cistercian churches, Fountains had no great bell-tower but simply a lantern at the crossing which had been causing concern since the late fourteenth century. Huby's first plan seems to have been to build a new crossing tower. His work can be identified by the widespread use of magnesian limestone, first used by Darnton, and the frequent use of his initials and motto. First the continuing weakness of the south-east crossing pier and the arch into the south presbytery aisle was addressed by underbuilding a substantial new arch carried on a reinforced timber raft (**67**), and then wide cracks in the failing masonry of the east wall of the south transept were repaired (**68**). However, Huby's masons, apparently led by Christopher Scune who had previously underbuilt the fallen central tower at Ripon, must have thought it better to abandon that scheme and consider a new tower elsewhere (**colour plate 9**).

The late fifteenth century was a period of tower-building in the north of England, and the Cumberland abbeys of Shap and Furness both built monu-

66 *Three fifteenth-century alabaster panels from an incomplete retable found at Fountains in the early nineteenth century. They illustrate scenes from the life of the Virgin: on the left the Assumption; in the centre the Coronation of the Virgin; and on the right the Nativity. All bear traces of polychrome decoration*

mental western towers to house peals of bells and to mark their status. Abbot Redman of Shap was the Bishop of Ely and Visitor of the English province of Premonstratensian canons, of comparable rank to Huby who was commissary to the abbot of Cîteaux. Huby chose unusually to build his new tower at the end of the north transept (**69**). The scale and design of this new tower amply demonstrates Fountains' importance as the pre-eminent Cistercian house in England and the status of Abbot Huby, that 'golden and unbreakable column in his zeal for the order'.

Huby's tower survives intact but for its floors, roof, bells, and some window tracery, 48.7m (160ft) high and of four stages. It was a tower designed to impress, rising from a deep moulded plinth and supported by massive angle buttresses. Externally, it was divided into four storeys by string-courses which correspond approximately to its internal floors, and is topped by an embattled parapet which originally had tall pinnacles at the angles, standing on the buttresses and connected to the wall head by miniature flying buttresses, with small pinnacles corbelled out from the parapet in middle of each side. The windows of each stage vary: the ground and second floors have standard Perpendicular traceried windows with pointed heads that would have matched closely Abbot Darnton's new windows in the church itself, the first floor had similar windows with elliptical heads, and the fourth floor had three-light windows with square heads. The bell-chamber occupied the third floor and its windows were closed with wooden louvers; otherwise all the windows were glazed.

67 *The timber raft that Huby insert-ed to support a new arch into the south presbytery aisle is clearly visible as voids in the clay and stone packing set around it*

68 *Huby's repair of the crossing required the insertion of a new arch into the south aisle of the presbytery and an alarming crack in the wall above appeared. The photograph, taken in the 1930s shows areas of twelfth century limewash which has now largely disappeared.*
English Heritage

69 *Huby's tower was built for show and remains a powerful reminder of both the abbot's and the abbey's power and influence.* English Heritage

The proportions of the tower are enhanced by its decoration. The angle buttresses have tall niches under gabled heads which were designed to take statues though none appear to have ever been fixed. Above seven of the windows are smaller niches, five of which retain statues. On the south face above the lowest window is the statue of an abbot without a mitre, perhaps St Bernard, while above the lowest window on the north face is St Catherine and above the second window St James the Great. The statues above the lowest windows on the east and west faces of the tower are angels holding shields, that on the east bearing the three horseshoes of Fountains, that on the west the mitre, staff, and initials of Huby himself. Bands of black-letter inscription 0.6m (2ft) high were placed below the parapet and the upper two tiers of windows, comprising Latin texts taken from the Cistercian breviary. The upper bands are badly eroded but still partly legible, the lowest reads: 'REGI AUTEM SAECULORUM IMMORTALI, INVISIBLI, SOLI DEO, HONOR ET GLORIA IN S(AECU)LA S(AECU)LOR(UM)' ('now unto the King Eternal, Immortal, Invisible, the Only God, be honour and glory for ever'), repeated four times with slight variation. It was from this verse, taken originally from St Paul's first epistle to Timothy, that Huby derived his personal motto 'Soli Deo honor et gloria' (only to God be the honour and glory) used on many of his buildings.

Within the church, Huby's hand can be seen in continuing improvements. A new pulpitum screen was provided between the second pair of piers in the nave and new choir stalls were provided for the thirty or so monks who now occupied the abbey. The stalls are gone, but were probably the work of the Bromflete family of Ripon who were providing new stalls and screenwork for the monks of Jervaulx (**colour plate 10**) and the canons of Bridlington and Easby at this time. Their site is marked by the stone-lined pits (now buried) which comprised a hollow space below the wooden floor of the stalls to give more resonance to the singing. This effect was further heightened in the northern bank of stalls by the inclusion of open-necked pottery jars in the stone lining of the pit. In the nave, Huby added statue brackets to the fourth pier from the west of the north arcade and fifth pier of the south arcade, and placed a series of limestone markers in the nave floor that indicated the positions to be taken by members of the community when they visited the nave on their Sunday procession.

Alterations to the infirmary

The monks' lives outside their church were also changing, and although the main cloister ranges remained unaltered there are indications that they were made more comfortable and less draughty. A smaller number of monks would permit the partitioning of the dormitory to provide more private cells for instance, but Fountains does not display the same degree of growing comfort in its cloister ranges that many monasteries do. Even in the sixteenth century,

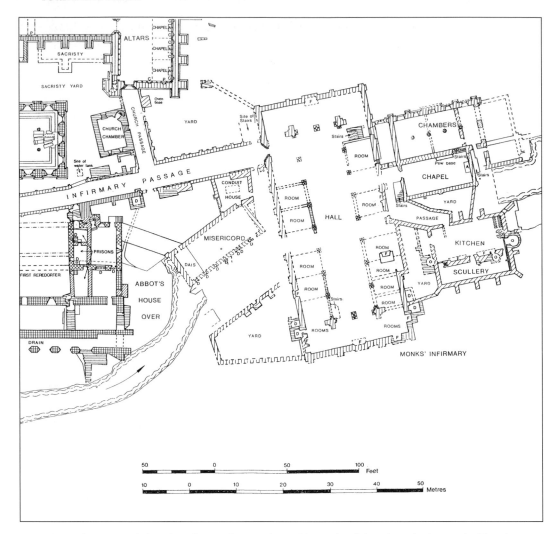

70 *In this section of plan, the infirmary shows evidence of being altered throughout the fourteenth, fifteenth, and sixteenth centuries as it became more and more the centre of monastic life at the expense of the cloister ranges*

Abbot William Thirsk was able to claim that the traditions of his 'religion' set apart the behaviour of his order from others. Substantial changes did occur at Fountains but not within the confines of the cloister, and it may be that the cloister buildings were all but abandoned for daily life by the late fifteenth century in favour of the infirmary (**70**).

The development of monastic life in the late thirteenth and fourteenth centuries can best be seen in the way the infirmary buildings were adapted. What had begun its life as a monastery within a monastery for the old and sick became an increasingly important element in the lives of the whole community.

In the late thirteenth century, the building to the north-east of the infirmary hall was converted to provide a home for Abbot Peter Ayling who resigned in

1279. At the same time, a new chapel was provided to the south, presumably replacing a smaller chapel provided by John of Kent. Ayling's house communicated by a mural stair with this chapel, enabling him to hear divine service while avoiding the community he had scandalised and nearly bankrupted by unwise speculation. The softer lifestyle of the infirmary was perhaps more to the taste of an ex-abbot than a return to the life of the cloister. Old and sick monks had always been allowed richer food than the rest of the community and this included both meat and eggs which were proscribed in the refectory. After 1300, the Benedictines relaxed their rule to permit the occasional eating of meat. The Cistercians were slow to follow them, but follow them they did, and by the late fourteenth century it was to the infirmary that they came to eat meat. The fourteenth century saw the building of a fine meat-kitchen to the south-east of the infirmary hall with two great fireplaces and a battery of ovens.

From the second half of the fourteenth century, the aisles of the infirmary hall were divided into a series of chambers by stone walls, a process that continued into the fifteenth century, providing a series of studies and bedrooms. These rooms were on two floors, evidenced by the remains of the staircases to an upper storey and by external latrine shafts that could not be entered from the ground floor in every case. Many of the rooms at ground-floor level had fireplaces. It was originally thought that these rooms were simply an improved version of the curtained cubicles that the old and sick were first provided with, and it is not a peculiarity of the infirmary at Fountains. Exactly the same process can be seen at Kirkstall, Waverley, Tintern, and Quarr. There is an alternative interpretation which is rapidly growing in currency, that these sets of rooms were bed-sits for individual monks, borrowing from the accommodation provided in colleges, the rapidly growing universities of Oxford and Cambridge (particularly in the monastic halls), and the individual cells provided for Carthusian monks. Nowhere is this more clearly seen than at Byland Abbey where the infirmary was swept away at the end of the thirteenth century to be replaced by a series of ten cells with fireplaces and latrines built from the reclaimed materials. It would appear that the senior monks at Fountains, like their brothers at Byland and elsewhere, had left the cloister ranges for more comfortable accommodation.

John Darnton provided the converted infirmary with a meat refectory or misericord in the late fifteenth century, replacing an earlier building with latrines, and connected it to his own house with a covered passage. Little now remains of this building but when it was excavated in the nineteenth century it was found to resemble a domestic hall with a raised dais at its west end and a service passage at its east end. The dais and floor were tiled and stone benches were placed along the side walls. A further wall bench was provided on the dais which was edged with limestone blocks decorated with small quatrefoils. This room served the convent as a small and comfortable dining room, still recognisable in its planning as a Cistercian refectory. Among the

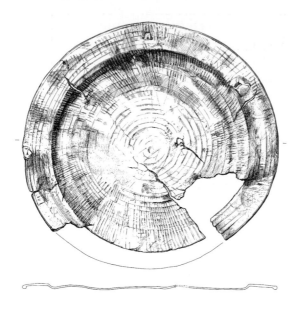

71 *A pewter plate found in rubbish dumped outside the misericord marked with a single horseshoe to demonstrate that it was the property of the abbey.* Judith Dobie

rubbish thrown out from it was a pewter plate, part of the garnish that must have occupied a dresser in the room (**71**).

The growth of the abbot's house

As the comfort of the choir-monks increased so did that of the abbot. His house, originally of modest proportions, was to grow substantially from the fourteenth century until it reached its greatest extent in the early sixteenth century (**72** & **colour plate 12**).

The growth of the abbot's house reflected the growth of his status both within and outside the monastery. Within the abbey, the abbot was, according to the Rule of St Benedict that the Cistercians followed, 'considered to represent the person of Christ' and was to be treated accordingly. As head of the community he had obligations outside the monastery, for the abbey had extensive estates and thus feudal responsibilities. The abbot of Fountains effectively enjoyed the status of an earl and as such could be summoned to Parliament. The first abbot to be so called was Robert Thornton between 1290 and 1296. The abbot was also likely to be called on to serve on commissions of the peace of his county and to collect taxes imposed by the Crown on ecclesiastical property. On the abbey's own estates he was responsible for the administration of justice. From the fourteenth century, the abbot of Fountains had additional external responsibilities as a mitred abbot, one of only three Cistercian abbots to be so honoured in England by the Pope. The granting of the mitre, ring, gloves and sandals, the insignia of a bishop, was only made to the heads of religious houses which were important enough and sufficiently wealthy to pay for such an honour. The

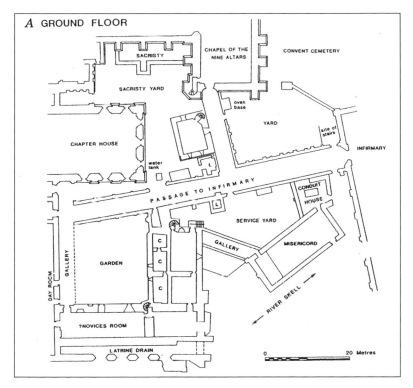

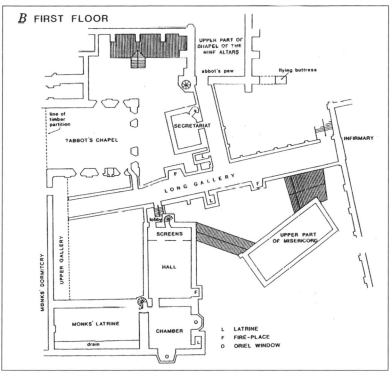

72 *A: the surviving remains of the abbot's house at ground floor level; B: the likely arrangement of the abbot's apartments at first floor level in the sixteenth century*

73 *The basement level of the abbot's house as it survives today contains on its west side three prison cells, each with its own latrine*

honour brought quasi-episcopal authority over a whole district and a seat in the House of Lords as one of the lords spiritual. It was not a mark of monastic spirituality but a recognition of high status within the church and outside. That status at Fountains was marked by a steady growth in the size of the abbot's household and the space given over to house it.

The earliest alterations to the house built by Richard of Clairvaux in the 1160s appear to belong to the abbacy of Walter Coxwold (1313-36). The ground floor had originally been a cellar and this he divided to provide a prison with three small cells on the west side (**73**), each with their own latrine, accessible from the small yard enclosed by the east range, the infirmary cloister, the abbot's cell, and the monks' latrine block. The remainder of the cellar was retained and Coxwold provided a newel stair down to it at the north end of his hall. Each cell had an iron staple in its floor for the prisoners' chains, showing that monastic discipline could be, and was, strictly enforced. When the southernmost cell was excavated in the mid-nineteenth century, Walbran found the words *vale libertas* (farewell liberty) scratched into the wall. A Latin inscription would suggest that the prison was used for monks rather than common felons.

The accommodation at first-floor level was substantially enlarged. The wall dividing the original hall and chamber was removed to create a new hall 16.2m long and 10m wide. The northernmost 3m comprised the screens passage, covering the entrance in the north wall and the stair to the basement. This new hall was further improved by having a wall-fireplace at the south end of its east wall. The base of the chimney stack survives, blocking a twelfth century door into the basement. A new chamber was created in the east end of the monks' latrine block, 10m square, with a latrine in its south-east corner discharging into the Skell. Later remodelling has removed virtually all trace of the fourteenth-century arrangements of this room. The scale of this enlarged abbot's house can be gauged by comparing it with the contemporary abbot's house at Jervaulx. There, the complete lodging measured only 12.6m by 5.5m, small enough to fit comfortably inside the abbot of Fountains' hall, though Jervaulx was far from being a poor house. It was, however, a daughter-house of Byland and therefore of secondary status. The abbot of Byland had a hall virtually the same size as his contemporary at Fountains.

Later in the fourteenth century, perhaps during the abbacy of William Gower, the abbot's house was again extended but in a rather unusual way. An upper floor was added to the infirmary cloister which required the partial blocking of the open arcades at ground-floor level, and the addition of new, deeper buttresses. Access to this new upper gallery was provided from the landing outside the north door of the abbot's hall. What purpose it served is uncertain, though the northern corridor might have led to the abbot's pew in the south gable of the Chapel of Nine Altars from which the abbot could hear services conducted in the southern chapel there. A bridge from the western arm of the gallery led to the area over the chapter-house which had originally formed part of the dormitory, and it was here that a private chapel was created for the abbot. A new window was inserted into the centre of the east wall of this space in the late fourteenth century.

It was Marmaduke Huby who was responsible for the final remodelling of the house though little of his work now remains. Excavation in the nine-teenth century recovered he remains of the fine square-headed windows in

74 *A limestone panel depicting the Annunciation of the Virgin, showing the Virgin standing to the right by a reading desk with a cranked stem, with a vase of lilies at the centre, and the Archangel Gabriel kneeling to the left. The scroll reads Ave M(a)ri(a), (Gracia) Plena, D(omi)n(u)s Tecu(m) (Hail Mary full of grace, the Lord be with you). A similar panel was placed over the door to the contemporary abbot's house at Rievaulx and this panel was almost certainly similarly placed.* English Heritage

75 *Part of the overmantle of a highly decorated fireplace, this stone bears the device of Marmaduke Huby. The initials 'm h' flank a crosier set within a mitre and are composed of intertwined dragons except for the upright stem of the h which is a hobby or small hawk that puns on the abbot's name. Above is a scroll that was originally painted with the abbot's motto Soli Deo Honor et Gloria.*
English Heritage

magnesian limestone that had lit his rooms. A limestone panel of the Annunciation of the Virgin removed from the site in the eighteenth century is so similar to that over the door to the abbot's house at Rievaulx that it probably occupied a similar position here (**74**). Excavation also recovered 'stones bearing the well-known initials MH', none of which can now be identified, but a similar panel from an elaborate overmantle recovered from a local cottage most probably came from the abbot's house (**75**). Work of Huby's time can be recognised in the basement of his great chamber at the south end of the house to which oriel windows were added, and in the infirmary cloister. Here great chimneys and latrine towers were added to both sides of the passage, and the fourteenth century upper storey must have been substantially rebuilt. It had become a long gallery where the abbot and his guests could exercise, an addition which was becoming fashionable in the greatest of private houses. To the north of this gallery remains the ground floor of a two-storey building that housed the abbot's secretariat, Huby's *nova camera versus ecclesiam* or 'church chamber' where so many of his leases were witnessed.

Although Marmaduke Huby was known in his lifetime as a reformer, the extent of his building works and those of his predecessors indicates how far Cistercian life had moved in four centuries. It was only the reformation of the English church in the 1530s that stopped the continuing development of Fountains, preserving so well the twelfth- and thirteenth-century buildings which were already becoming redundant.

5

AGRICULTURE, INDUSTRY AND WEALTH

Fountains, in common with the majority of medieval monasteries, depended on an agricultural and industrial estate for the support of the community and the financing of its building campaigns. Exceptionally, Archbishop Thurstan had omitted to provide the substantial landed endowment that normally accompanied the foundation of a religious house, and the monks were therefore obliged to build up an estate as best they could. Their success in this venture was one of the most remarkable in the history of the monastic church.

The nature and extent of the estate

At the foundation, Hugh of Kirkstall tells us that Archbishop Thurstan provided the community with two carucates (about 105ha) of cultivated land at Sutton to the north of Ripon and 81ha in the wood of Herleshowe to the south of the abbey for their support. Some of this land was actually the gift of the archbishop's tenant, Wallef FitzArkill, and Thurstan was doing little more than confirming that gift. From that small and inadequate beginning, it was only the monks' reputation for strict and spiritual living and their abbots' administrative skills that were to persuade the land-owning classes to grant the lands for their sustenance. In the earliest years, when failure seemed likely, they were initially reluctant to part even with moorland that was marginal to their own estates. Once established, however, it was a different story, with the great northern families, the Mowbrays, the Percys, the Romellis, and the earls of Richmond vying to surpass each others' generosity. Although the abbey's estates were broken up in the 1540s it is possible to reconstruct their extent from a number of sources, starting in the last years of the abbey's life and working backwards (**76**).

Two surviving documents are central to understanding the nature and extent of Fountains' landholdings: a collection of the abbey's charters and confirmations made for Marmaduke Huby in the last years of the fifteenth century, bound up in five volumes (one is missing but its contents can be recovered from an earlier cartulary); and the survey of the monastery's income made in 1535 for the *Valor*

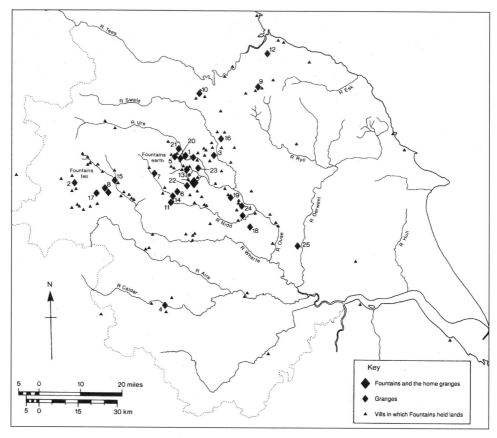

76 *The landholdings of Fountains Abbey. For the most part the abbeys estates lay in Yorkshire, though there were also substantial holdings in Cumbria. Many of the symbols on this map conceal substantial holdings. The granges are: 1 Alburgh; 2 Arnfold; 3 Baldersby; 4 Bradley; 5 Bramley; 6 Brimham; 7 Bouthwaite; 8 Bordely; 9 Busby; 10 Cowton; 11 Dacre; 12 Eston; 13 Galphay; 14 Heyshaw; 15 Kilnsey; 16 Kirby Wiske; 17 Malham; 18 Marston; 19 Marton; 20 Nutwith; 21 Pott; 22 Sawley, 23 Sutton; 24 Thorpe Underwood; 25 Wheldrake*

Ecclesiasticus (see Chapter Six). Taken together, an impressive picture can be reconstructed of the lands owned by the abbey and their respective values in the late Middle Ages. In all, Fountains had an interest in 138 vills, ranging from the holding of a single tenement to the whole of the manor. In 1535, the taxable income from these individual holdings ranged from 1s (5p) to £111 6s 8d (£111.33), and the total net taxable income of the estate was some £1115, making Fountains the richest house of the order in England. Fountains' income had grown to four times that of its rival Rievaulx.

The Cistercian approach to estate management

From their earliest years, the Cistercians rejected the normal sources of monastic revenue: churches with their tithes, manors held by feudal tenure, mills and rents, for these did not 'accord with monastic purity' and contact with laymen distracted the monks from their devotions. Instead, they chose to accept gifts of land that they could manage directly themselves with great armies of lay brothers who were subject to monastic discipline. Yorkshire in the twelfth century was ideal territory for Cistercian expansion. The Yorkshire Domesday survey of 1086 shows that out of 1500 villages in the county 850 were totally depopulated and a further 400 had severely reduced populations because of the Danish raids that followed the conquest of England in 1066 and King William's harrying of the north after abortive rebellions. The precise situation is still far from understood and the population of the county must have begun to recover before 1130, but it is fair to assume that large parts of Yorkshire and particularly the marginal uplands were still substantially under-populated. For an order which sought isolation from the world this was an ideal situation.

The key to Cistercian land-management was the grange or estate centre which might lie at a considerable distance from the abbey and which provided a focus for a particular block of land. Staffed by lay brothers, it was a self-contained unit supported by outlying lodges and could exploit a mixed economy. Granges, like the abbeys of the order, were required to be in unpopulated areas to prevent 'contamination' by the outside world. This helped the Cistercians to maintain their policy of centralised farming which cut across the traditional (and less efficient) agricultural economy of the countryside. Where the local arrangement did not suit this method existing populations would be ruthlessly evicted if they got in the way of the grange system. It was not a policy which made the Cistercians popular though it added to their wealth, and Fountains was no exception, depopulating the vills of Cayton, Greenberry, and Thorpe Underwood to create estate centres. Some granges had specialist functions, for instance the breeding of horses and cattle. Others were the centres of great sheep runs or were industrial in nature. They functioned as a network, one communicating with another, and all communicating with the abbey at the centre. The concept was remarkably simple and highly centralised, depending for its success on the right grants of land from patrons and a good supply of well-motivated lay brothers. In the twelfth century, both were freely available and enabled the order to exploit land in a way which had not been possible since the last years of the Roman empire. Indeed, the model for this approach could have been the Roman Imperial estates themselves.

Few medieval buildings survive today on any of the Fountains granges, only the gatehouse range at Kilnsey (**77**), the chapel at Bewerley, and a barn at Sutton; only one, Cowton Grange has been excavated. There, substantial timber-framed buildings on cobbled footings had been replaced by smaller-scale domestic buildings in the fourteenth century. However, there are pointers to the early Cistercian granges in England. At Laskill, a home grange of Rievaulx, traces remain of a great stone building with evidence for a vaulted ground floor, every bit as substantial as the cloister ranges of the abbey, built

77 *The gatehouse range at Kilnsey was rebuilt in the late fourteenth century.* Judith Roebuck

perhaps in the 1160s making it contemporary with the core buildings of the monastery itself. Being out-stations for the lay brothers it would be reasonable to expect the distant granges to resemble miniature monasteries with living accommodation and a chapel as well as barns, storehouses, animal houses, and industrial buildings. The Fountains grange of Malham had a piped water supply similar to that of the monastery itself, installed before 1190-1210 which implies a high degree of organisation. In France, that degree of organisation can still be seen in surviving buildings such as the Chaalis granges of Vaulerent and Foucheret and the Pontigny granges of le Beugnon, Crécy, and Villiers-le-Grange. In England, the principal survivor is the vast barn on the Beaulieu grange of Great Coxwell. A grange or supporting lodge was not simply a group of buildings but also the infrastructure of arable fields, meadows, pasture, and woodland, substantial traces of which remain today. In upland Yorkshire, the Fountains lay brothers substantially altered the twelfth-century landscape and much of it remains in the state that they left it.

The early Cistercians went about their estate management with the same certainty that drove their spiritual lives. The self-confidence with which they exploited marginal land and developed its administration made them both agricultural and industrial innovators. It comes as no surprise to find that their libraries contained books on agriculture such as the twelfth-century copy of Palladius' *Opus Agriculture* that belonged to Byland Abbey and still survives. The success of the order and the wealth that provided its monumental buildings resulted directly from the way in which they exploited their estates. The ability of an abbey to attract land-grants in its formative years and the election of abbots who were skilful administrators as well as spiritual leaders would together ensure that the house developed and sustained a sound economy, guaranteeing its survival and its undisturbed round of prayer. This was the secret of Fountains' success in the twelfth and thirteenth centuries.

The development of an estate and its exploitation

After the recorded gifts of the founder Archbishop Thurstan, the first indication of the development of the abbey's estates is found in a confirmation of land gifts acknowledged by King Stephen in 1135 at the point at which the abbey was about to achieve *stabilitas*. At that stage, the abbey held Thurstan's gifts of Sutton and Hereleshowe, and two carucates at Cayton in two parcels of land, the gift of Eustace FitzJohn of Knaresborough. A second confirmation issued by Stephen before 1152 and after Thurstan's death in 1140 — the period which saw the building and rebuilding of the first stone monastery — unhelpfully gives no details of the lands granted from the York archiepiscopal estates by Henry Murdac, and by Earl Alan of Richmond and other faithful barons. For the growth of the abbey estates in that critical period we have to look elsewhere. A confirmation of Pope Eugenius issued in 1146 lists granges at Sutton, Cayton, Cowton Moor, Warsill, Dacre, and Aldburgh, in addition to further lands in Rainborough, New Hall, and Troutsdale as well as those lands given by Eustace FitzJohn 'for the building of the abbey'. A similar grant, known only from the cartulary, was made by Adam FitzSwain in 1145. The building of permanent stone ranges for the monks was thus paralleled by the organisation of the abbey's land-holdings into a fully developed grange system, and perhaps Henry Murdac's hand should be seen in this.

From existing charters, most of which are remarkably difficult to date accurately, it is possible to see how the estates were assembled from many individual grants. The two principal periods of acquisition appear to be in the late 1140s and 1150s and from 1174 to 1185. Amongst the earliest were those of Robert de Sartis and his wife Raganild who gave lands in Bishop Thornton for an annual rent of 6s 8d (33p) and who sold the monk's Gill Moor where they had established a sheep-run before 1136. That land was not an outright gift indicates that the convent was seeking land rather than simply being given it, and at such an early date when the convent was in no position to fund its own purchases, some of the earliest donations must have been of cash. Robert and his wife also rented land at Warsill to the convent for half a mark of silver (33p) which they later gave the community, perhaps a form of hire purchase, and which was coupled with the grant of three carucates at Herleshowe. The land at Warsill remained until 1539 the basis of the early grange there: 195ha of pasture, meadows, and woods.

More complex was the assembly of lands in Nidderdale to the south of the abbey. Bertram Haget, the father of the later Abbot Ralph and a tenant of the

Mowbrays, gave the community lands valued at two marks (£1.33), a substantial holding compared with Warsill, on which the grange of Dacre was established as early as 1138. Some years later, Roger de Mowbray, the most generous of Fountains' benefactors and the founder of Byland Abbey, added to his tenant's grant and allowed the grange to be relocated on better land that he had farmed himself. He also gave mineral rights in the forest of Nidderdale to the monks, and in 1174 granted the monks the greater part of the forest itself. In 1175, he added further to the monks' holding in Nidderdale. In the same year he lost a substantial part of his estates as a result of his involvement in an abortive rebellion against Henry II, and consequently, Fountains lost lands held from Roger south of Dacre. Roger was obliged to compensate the monks by granting additional land (for a payment) on Dallow Moor on the east side of Nidderdale and a few days later all of his holdings at Lofthouse. Earl Roger's disgrace was to Fountains' advantage, for having lost royal favour he decided to seek safety in pilgrimage to Jerusalem. This was an expensive business and Roger turned to Fountains for assistance, selling the abbey land to the value of £450. Though there is no evidence that he actually went to Jerusalem at the time, he was later to go on crusade and die a captive of the Saracens in 1188. By the end of the twelfth century the greater part of upper Nidderdale was in Fountains' hands.

From William de Percy came vast estates in Craven granted before 1174. This included all the pasture of Malham Moor, and Malham Tarn with its important fishery. William's tenants Thurstan de Arches and Ulf FitzRoskill provided further grants of land around Malham, making this area a major estate in its own right. His daughter Matilda, Countess of Warwick, continued her father's benefaction, giving further lands in Malham and the forest of Langstroth, to which her sister and co-heiress Agnes, wife of Jocelin de Louvain, added. Later Percys were to regret the munificence of their forebears and were to challenge unsuccessfully Fountains' rights to many estates in the courts. The outcome of these disputes was that Fountains' holdings were confirmed and further endowments were offered. Richard de Percy, as a grant to persuade the monks to accept his body for burial in the mid-thirteenth century, gave the abbey the whole of the vill of Litton in Craven with the forest of Littondale, an area which had been in dispute for three generations. Richard's son, Henry, disputed this settlement and it was not until 1297 and the payment of 600 marks of silver (£400) by the abbey that Fountains had secure title to this land. It can be seen from the surviving agreements and court rolls that the building up of so extensive an estate was both slow and complicated, requiring so great an overview that the abbey must have been working to a blueprint from its earliest years.

Between 1203 and 1265, a considerable effort was made to consolidate the abbey's lands, renting out areas that were not easily farmed in hand and acquiring parcels of land that complemented areas already held, either by exchange or purchase. Agreements were reached with both Rievaulx and Byland that neither would act to the disadvantage of Fountains as they carried out the same exercise, and with other monasteries where it was felt necessary. Such prior agreement did not always work and Fountains found itself having to take legal action against other monks to protect its interests. Such was the competition for land that Fountains found itself accusing the abbot and convent of Furness of forgery and perjury in their attempt to secure disputed holdings in Craven in the early fourteenth century. Fountains was not above dubious practice either, for at the end of the thirteenth century the monks enclosed a highway at Wheldrake that prevented access to land held by Warter Priory there. In this case, Fountains was forced to make amends and provide a new road. The resulting agreement shows that the canons of Warter held a deep mistrust of Fountains' monks which resulted from a history of high-handedness.

By 1265, Fountains' holdings had reached their maximum extent and represented a highly organised and profitable estate that was not entirely confined to Yorkshire. There were few granges at great distance from the abbey, and all were strategically placed as staging posts to link distant holdings with the abbey itself. In this way, the grange of Baldersby to the north-east of Fountains provided the first link in the chain of estate centres that ran through Kirby Wiske to Cowton in the Vale of Mowbray and Busby in Cleveland. Similarly, Marton and Thorpe Underwood were stages on the journey to York and the important range of Wheldrake on the Derwent, a route which also passed through Hammerton and Marston. Substantial though the landholdings to the east were, the main body of Fountains' lands lay on the higher ground to the west, extending in a virtually unbroken sweep from the west gates of the abbey into Lancashire and Cumberland.

To the north of the abbey were the home granges of Swanley, Galphay and Sutton, to the south-west Warsil, and to the south Morker (or Hereleshowe), Haddockstanes and Cayton. Beyond these, further granges were set on the floor of the dales that reach up into the Pennines. Lower Wensleydale was managed from Sleningfold, while the upper reaches were administered from Aldburgh and Nutwith. Pott grange lay on the flank of Colsterdale, and Bramley at the head waters of the River Laver. Lower Nidderdale was served by Dacre and the lodges of Brimham, Bewerley and Heyshaw, and the upper dale by Bouthwaite and the lodge of Lofthouse. Huge tracts of land on the east side of the dale were held by Fountains on Dallow Moor and Fountains Earth Moor above Bouthwaite grange. Kilnsea served upper Wharfedale (**78**) and Arncliffe served Littondale. These granges were in turn serviced by the lodges of Foxup, Cosh, Upper and Lower Heseldon and Fornagill which were tucked into the narrow ghylls that provided access to the high moors. Fountains Moor on the south flank of Pen-y-Ghent bears testimony to the abbey's sheep-runs there. Malham and the twin granges of Bordley lay in Craven, off the headwaters of Airedale, with Arnfold planted in Ribblesdale,

78 *The grange of Kilnsea in upper Wharfedale retains substantial earthworks that mark the closes, barns, granaries and droveways, an indication of the scale at which the Fountains granges were laid out.* English Heritage

controlling vast areas of pasture and arable land. Malham Moor was good sheep and cattle territory, and the abbey's *bercariae* and *vaccariae* with their pastures, droves, buildings and animal pens can still be traced in the earthworks that extend across the landscape there (**79**).

Only two granges lay outside this closely woven net, Bradley near Huddersfield on the Calder, and Allerdale in Cumberland. From these farflung estates wayleaves had been negotiated for the moving of stock over other people's land. At Bradley, a holding of 1780ha had been assembled in the late twelfth century. The grange was established by 1193 and by 1194 the abbey was operating a forge there producing iron. Bradley was made up of a series of small grants in the townships of Huddersfield and Kirk Heaton, the extents of which can be ascertained from surviving charter evidence (**80**). There is evidence to suggest that Fountains had targeted the area because of its industrial potential, and as parcels of land were acquired, wayleaves between them were negotiated in a way which suggests the monks were acting to a masterplan that would give them access to iron ore, timber, and watercourses, all essential if a forge was to be established. The monks of Rievaulx were acquiring similar provisions at Flockton and Wombwell in the 1160s and 70s, as were Byland at its granges of Bentley and Denby and Bordesley at its grange of Lye in Worcestershire. As well as being pioneers of agriculture the Cistercians were also in the forefront of industrial development. They were not alone in this endeavour, however, for at the same period the important

Augustinian house of Guisborough was developing ironworks in Eskdale. The production of iron was a highly profitable venture.

At Bradley, evidence for ironworking survives in the largely rural area of Kirkheaton in the valley of Smythclough where substantial earthworks and scatters of ironworking debris and slag indicates the site of perhaps the earliest identified water-powered industrial complex in medieval England. Bradley's economy was not, however, predominantly industrial, although it does include a pottery production site of the thirteenth and fourteenth centuries at Upper (or Potter) Heaton where monastic exploitation of a traditional peasant industry to serve the Fountains properties in this part of West Yorkshire can be assumed. The grange also had cattle and sheep, and the presence of a mill implies extensive

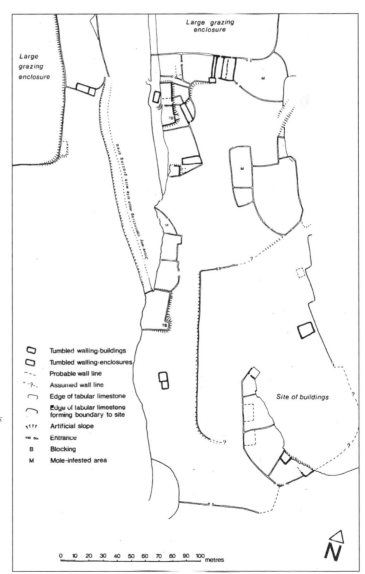

79 *The earthwork remains of Bolton Priory's sheep run or bercary on Abbot Hills above Malham, a property disputed by Fountains, lie at the centre of extensive stone-walled grazing enclosures. Fountains' own lodges in the area differ little in their layout.*
Steve Moorhouse

Legend:
- Tumbled walling·buildings
- Tumbled walling·enclosures
- Probable wall line
- Assumed wall line
- Edge of tabular limestone
- Edge of tabular limestone forming boundary to site
- Artificial slope
- Entrance
- B Blocking
- M Mole-infested area

Large grazing enclosure

Large grazing enclosure

Site of buildings

0 10 20 30 40 50 60 70 80 90 100 metres

N

111

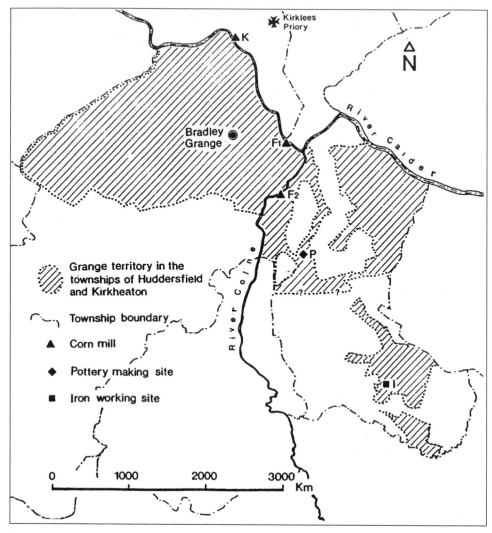

80 *The lands of Bradley grange can be reconstructed from charter evidence. K marks the site of the Kirklees Priory mill; F1 the site of the proposed Fountains mill; F2 its final location; P the site of the Upper Heaton pottery production site; and I the ironworks of Smythclough.* Steve Moorhouse

arable farming. The mill itself had a remarkable history which is perhaps typical of the problems even large monasteries faced in organising their estates. Fountains entered into a series of agreements with its neighbours in order to build a mill on the River Calder. The poor Cistercian nuns of Kirklees controlled the north bank of the Calder and built their own mill above the Fountains site, depriving the proposed mill of an uninterrupted water supply. Although Fountains had shown itself to be willing in other cases to use its might to overawe lesser houses, in this case the monks seem to have been unwilling to take on the prioress of Kirklees and chose instead to build their mill on the Colne where they controlled both banks of the river.

In the twelfth and thirteenth centuries, Fountains income was substantially derived from the wool-trade, using the proceeds to finance building both within the precinct and on the granges and lodges, and to buy land (which was technically forbidden by the statutes of the order). By 1300, the abbey ran some 15,000 sheep and revenue from the sale of wool was three times that from all other sources. The wool-trade has tended to overshadow the abbey's other interests which were as extensive as they were varied. There were substantial fisheries on Derwentwater and Malham Tarn, on the Rivers Swale and Wiske, on the Rivers Ure and Ouse between Boroughbridge and York, and on the River Derwent at Wheldrake. Several granges also practised fish culture, their ponds still being traceable. Sea fishing was exploited off Teesmouth. They had resources to meet other needs too. Stone slates for roofing and stone for building were quarried in Craven, Nidderdale, Skelldale, and on Hutton Moor. Millstones were similarly quarried at Sawley and at Crossland near Huddersfield. Lead and iron were mined and refined in Nidderdale, and timber for building and for fuel was available across the estate.

Urban properties

Although the General Chapter of the order had ruled in 1134 that monks were not to live in towns, this does not seem to have particularly bothered the Fountains community who were assembling urban properties of varying extent in the towns of Boston, Yarm, Grimsby, Scarborough, York, Ripon and Doncaster. With the exception of the last two, all the towns targeted were ports and the purpose of establishing a presence there was trade as the abbey practised a surplus economy. Boston and York were the principal ports for the export of wool, first to Flanders and later to Italy, and the abbey's involvement there is understandable. Holdings in Grimsby, Scarborough, Redcar and Yarm provided access to the markets there, particularly for the purchase of sea fish that made up a substantial element of the monks' diet.

In Boston, the principal property lay in Wormgate where it is still marked by Fountains Lane. It was primarily used during the great fair of St Botulph as the headquarters of the abbey's agents. First granted before 1200 by Jordan de Boston, it was gradually expanded to include two mills in an area called *le poll*. A second property lay in Emery Lane on the west bank of the Witham, adjacent to a property held by the prior of Thornholme who acted as an agent for many of the smaller Lincolnshire monasteries in the wool-trade. It was enlarged by the acquisition of a second tenement in 1248. The bulk of the Fountains urban property was in York were acquisitions began in the 1170s and included a house with a resident caretaker and cook to provide for the officers of the abbey when they were in the city on business. The York properties were mainly on land close to the river and were so organised as to provide a major outlet for the abbey's wool exports. In 1224, the abbey owned its own ship licensed to carry wool, a privilege shared with its daughter-house of Kirkstall that indicates the level of investment made in the wool business. Properties not so well placed were leased out for a cash income.

The home granges

The abbey itself was ringed by a series of home granges whose purpose was to provide a focus for the more distant estates. They were principally the first granges to be established, with one important exception. They conducted the business that was either too noisy or unpleasant to be carried out inside the precinct itself, and they contained the animal houses and barns that are usually found within the precinct in other orders. They also acted as home farms producing the convents immediate food needs. To the north of Fountains lay Sutton grange, based on Thurstan's first gift of land and a grange by 1146. Roger de Mowbray and his tenants gave additional lands, and before 1156 the monks were keeping cattle there. By 1185 the grange had achieved the extent recorded by the suppression commissioners in 1539, lying astride the Kex Beck over which the monks had two bridges. Within the grange, the monks established a major pottery production site at Winksley in the late twelfth century.

Four kilns have been excavated and large quantities of the pottery produced have been recovered. This pottery has a very interesting distribution, being extremely rare in the market town of Ripon which is only 6.4km away and where it would have been marketed if it was intended for sale. Instead, it is found predominantly south and west of the kiln-site and particularly at Fountains Abbey itself. The pottery produced is distinctive (**81**), for while the fabric and forms used are derived from those of the contemporary Scarborough pottery industry (in which Fountains probably had an interest), the wedge-shaped rouletted decoration is copied from the Dutch pottery industry at Aardenburg. The Winksley kilns were established to serve the abbey and its home granges, yet a further example of the self-sufficiency of the Cistercian grange system and the internationalism of the order. The kilns remained in production until the last quarter of the thirteenth century, producing not only pottery, but the roof tiles used on the abbey buildings.

To the south of the abbey lay two extensive granges, those of Morker and Haddockstanes. The earthworks of the central enclosure of Morker remain at Nineveh Farm on the south side of the abbey precinct and the remains of a wall can still be seen on the western boundary of the grange. A gate in the precinct wall provided direct access to the outer court of the abbey itself. Between the grange buildings and the precinct wall were between 1 and 2ha of fishponds and there is slight evidence of stock compounds. To the west and enclosed by the 'Monks' Wall' was the grange of Haddockstanes, extending as far as the south bank of the River Skell. To the south of both lay Warsill, providing Fountains with a substantial farming capacity. Haddockstanes included part of the wood of Herleshowe and the surviving chapel of St Michael on Howe Hill. It also included a massive complex of four groups of fish ponds covering 16ha at Park House Farm. When these were recorded by Roy Gilyard-Beer in the late 1950s, each group of four ponds arranged around a square enclosure had the associated earthwork remains of a stone-built smoking house for the curing of fish. Only one group of ponds now remains in a recognisable state, but the degree of organisation is still apparent.

Perhaps the most remarkable of the home granges was that of Swanley adjoining the abbey precinct on the north. As with most of the other estates it had been assembled from a series of grants, but here the process of assembly belongs exceptionally to the thirteenth century. Alan de Aldfield acknowledged the gifts of his ancestors and granted a further area of land in 1272, providing the abbey with a block of land that extended from the brow of the

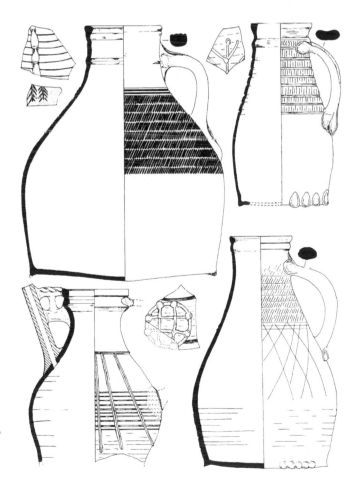

81 *Pottery from the kiln-site at Winksley on Sutton Grange. As well as decorated jugs, the Winksley potters also made cooking pots and bowls, and roof-tiles for the abbey buildings.* Jean le Patourel

hill overlooking the abbey on the north down to the River Skell. The grants concern land in the present-day parishes of Aldfield and Lindrick with Studley Royal and Fountains, from the valley of the Kendal to the north to the precinct wall and the river to the south, and from the parish boundary of Aldfield to the west to the Skell valley on the east (**82**), some 58ha of arable, pasture, and wood. The land was not formally farmed as a grange before 1300 but a confirmation of the earlier gifts of land by John de Mowbray in April 1317 provides a likely date for its inception.

The early fourteenth century was a troubled time for monasteries in the north of England, and Fountains was no exception, for the disastrous defeat of the English at Bannockburn had left the north of England open to Scots raiding to the extent that the walled city and castle of York were felt to be insecure. In 1318, many of the Fountains estates were overrun by the Scots, their buildings burned and contents looted, and the general spirit of lawlessness that pervaded the north made recovery difficult. The supply of lay brothers, traditionally raised from the abbey estates, had also been reduced to a trickle and the abbey was obliged to reconsider the way it organised its estates. The means chosen required the removal of some activities from granges that were no longer directly farmed being brought into the abbey itself. As the Fountains precinct was small, 30ha compared with the 40ha of Rievaulx, the development of an additional home grange in the early fourteenth century seems to have been the answer, and there can be little surprise that Swanley Grange was connected to the inner court of the monastery just within the inner gatehouse by a road that is still used as the entrance to the site from the modern visitor centre at Swanley.

The economy of Fountains in the later Middle Ages

Deprived of lay brothers, Fountains was no longer able to consider farming its estates in hand and three options were open to the convent. The granges could be run by hired workmen under the control of a bailiff, they could be leased to secular tenants for a cash rent, or depopulated vills could be repopulated and farmed on a feudal basis. Each option was counter to the twelfth century statutes and would compromise the very centralisation which had made the abbey so successful and powerful. Times had changed, though, and Fountains was not alone in being faced with the need to reform its economy. Most monasteries took the easy choice of tenanting the greater part of their estates and living off rents. Fountains, cushioned by its wealth, was able to take a longer view and set about a comprehensive review of its holdings and their management.

Workable granges were staffed by hired labour and remained in hand under the control of 10 bailiffs, serving Slenningfold and Galphay, Craven,

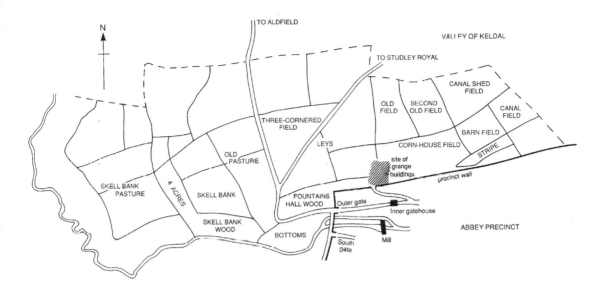

82 *The grange at Swanley can be reconstructed from its land grants which remained identifiable as fields on the tythe map of 1844.* After Judith Roebuck with additions

Nidderdale, Stainburn, Wheldrake, Hartwith, Grantley and Dalaghy, Aldburgh, Cowton and Greenberry, and Thorpe Underwood. An eleventh bailiff was appointed to manage the outer court of the monastery itself. In 1336, Abbot Coxwold leased those granges damaged in the wars to tenants, but not on a simple rental basis. Leasing had been allowed by the General Chapter in 1208 and Fountains had used leases as a way of managing land that was not central to its estates from the late twelfth century. The new tenants were not free to farm the lands as they wished, and might better be described as managers, for they were required to wear the abbot's livery and owed him feudal service. From the leases that survive, it is clear that the stock they farmed was the property of the abbey, and if a cow died the abbey would replace it on the production of its hide at the abbey's tannery. Tenants were required to bring their stock annually to the abbey where it was slaughtered, preventing its disposal on the open market. Finally, Abbot Robert Monkton began the conversion of granges into populated manors in 1363, effectively reversing the abbey's earlier policy of depopulation. By the early years of the fifteenth century there was little difference between the management of Fountains' estates and those of any other major monastery.

The conversion of the estates to lay management, while it was done in a way that exerted central control, undoubtedly had a marked effect on the landscape. Many of the smaller bercaries and vaccaries were abandoned, and granges were remodelled to suit their changed management. Gone were many of the great stone buildings, to be replaced by smaller timber structures more suited to their new uses. At Cowton, for instance, the large timber buildings of the twelfth century were replaced by a more domestic hall, chamber, and kitchen, of a scale more commonly found on lay manorial sites and which were more appropriate for a tenant or bailiff. The abbey itself appears to have provided these buildings, for tenancy agreements invariably contain a statement that the tenant was responsible for all repairs to the buildings but that the abbey was responsible for the provision of 'large timbers and stone thack (slates)' which were supplied from the estate.

The outer court of the monastery

All parts of the precinct that lay on the south side of the River Skell comprised the outer or base court of the abbey, an area given over to agricultural and

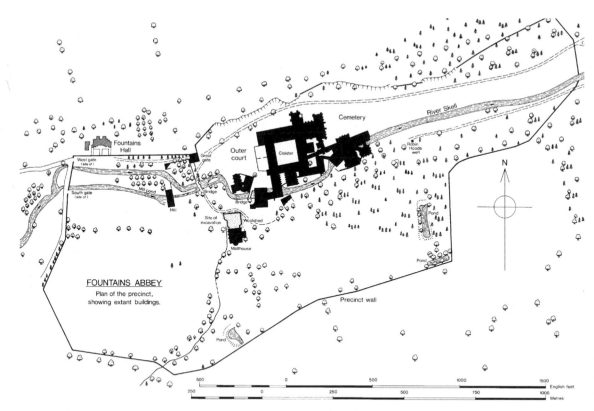

83 *The precinct of Fountains Abbey enclosed by its thirteenth-century wall and ringed by its home granges. The outer court comprised all of the land to the south of the River Skell. Only extant buildings are shown here*

industrial processes on which the life of the house depended (**83**). It had its own gate to the outside world, the South Gate, somewhat confusingly set in the west wall of the precinct, and a gate into Morker Grange on the south side. Today, the outer court survives largely as earthworks, but parts of two buildings survive, the mill and the woolhouse, and a third building, the tannery, was still standing in 1540 when the site was being offered for sale. The location of the tannery is no longer known but it must have been close to the river to the south and west of the guest house complex for it would have needed a regular water supply. Excavation in the 1880s by William St John Hope has identified a further building, the bake house and brew house, immediately to the south of the woolhouse. A study of the landscape has revealed the sites of a further 21 buildings all with associated yards and a network of roads that link them one to another. There are almost certainly more buildings that remain untraced. None of these buildings has been excavated or can be tied to documents that identify them, and there is as yet no evidence that they are all contemporary though they must all be monastic. Additionally there are large areas of land that contain no evidence of buildings but appear to have been cultivated as they bear slight evidence of ridge-and-furrow ploughing, areas of pasture for the animals kept in the precinct.

The outer court was the public area of the monastery as well as the centre of the monastic estate. It was the one area where women were permitted regular access, and at least one lived here, for the wife of the keeper of the south gate was employed as the convent's laundress. We have to look to Rievaulx to see what buildings lay here, for the late medieval layout of that abbey is remarkably well documented. Associated with the bake house and brew house was a kiln house or grain dryer and a series of granaries; associated with the tannery were the bark store, bark mill, lime kiln, and tannery barn; and associated with the corn mill were two others, a walk mill or fulling mill, and a water-powered smithy. There were houses for the convent smith and plumber, both resident in the outer court, and there was the common stable for general use of the precinct and guests. The swine house and its offices lay inside the outer court, for pig meat was an important element of the late medieval monastic diet. Each of these buildings was associated with a garth or yard. What would not be in the outer court of a major Cistercian abbey, as Rievaulx proves, were the great animal houses and barns that other orders enclosed within the precinct. At Rievaulx these were placed in the home granges that ringed the precinct, and some of the pasture land in the precinct was actually assigned to a home grange. There was, in fact, only an administrative difference between the outer court and the granges, and the dividing wall had more to do with accountability than security.

If the world of the cloister was quiet and controlled, the outer court was very different, a hive of noisy activity that sustained the convent throughout the year. Originally the province of the lay brothers, from the fourteenth century it would have been staffed by laymen, hired servants responsible to a bailiff, many of whom would have lived within the precinct. At Rievaulx, and probably at Fountains too, retired tenants and senior servants also lived in tied houses in the court, their food, drink, and fuel provided by the abbey. At the suppression it is likely that Fountains had at least 150 paid servants whose duties lay outside the cloister. Rievaulx had 104.

The centre of 'industrial' activity was a deep ghyll that ran down the hillside (**84**) with groups of buildings on terraces to the east and west, with the brew and bake house and the woolhouse, the latter the largest single building in the outer court, at its northern end. The powerful steam that ran down the ghyll provided the power to drive small mills, and building 72 that stood astride the stream was quite possibly served by a water wheel. To the west of the ghyll were three areas of pasture, 8, 9, and 19, each containing associated buildings (14, 15, 11, and 12), probably stables and byres. At some stage, the pasture had been reorganised and sub-divided by an earthen bank and a road (18). To the east of the ghyll were two areas known in the early sixteenth century as East and West Applegarths which approximate to two areas of pasture (131 and 110). East Applegarth lay adjacent to Pondgarth, which in turn contained a series of deep tanks (140, 142, and 147) which supplied water to the cloister ranges by way of a surviving well house, Robin Hood's Well, on the south bank of the Skell. A similar tank (52) to the west of West Applegarth supplied the lay brothers' quarters with piped water. The complexity of the outer court

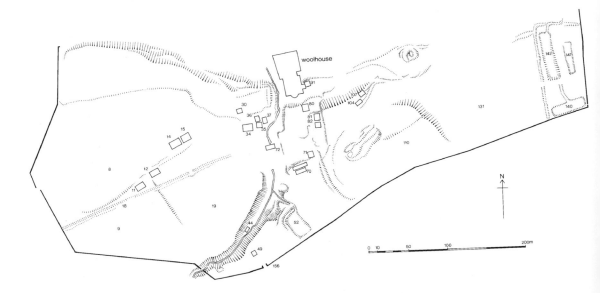

84 *The outer court is defined by a series of prominent earthworks which can be identified as the sites of buildings (shown in black outline), garths, roadways, and open areas that show evidence of cultivation. The precinct wall is shown as a continuous black line; the gaps are the location of gates*

85 *The surviving water mill, repaired and now open to the public, is one of the finest monastic mills in Europe. Operational until 1937 it is also the oldest surviving mill in Europe*

is similar to Rievaulx, with more or less the same buildings, and its scale is commensurate with the extent of the Fountains estate and home granges. Only excavation will demonstrate the true nature of the buildings it contained. The buildings that survive above ground had a complex development over four centuries and it is likely that those still buried were the same. It is from an examination of the surviving buildings that the scale and quality of all the outer court buildings can be gauged.

The mill (**85**) is the finest and oldest surviving example of a monastic corn mill in Europe; it appears to be an early thirteenth-century building that contains earlier masonry. A close examination of its masonry and some small-scale excavation in the course of its recent repair for display has enabled its complicated history to be unravelled for the first time, revealing no fewer than three distinct buildings (**86**). The earliest building, represented by its standing west and south walls and a short length of its excavated west wall, dates from the 1130s or 40s and was part of the first stone monastery. Windows survive in its east and south walls, that in the east wall having a monolithic head typical of early building at Fountains, and the east wall stands to full height. The mill race passed through its southern end, and the building had been destroyed in a flood that had pushed in its west wall, presumably in the 1150s when the building was reconstructed. This mill was buried in a new mill dam to prevent its successor suffering the same fate and the new building was constructed on top of its predecessor and the dam, now fed by a pond which could be more

EAST ELEVATION: medieval masonry

after Reeve
1892

after Reeve
1892

datum

after Reeve
1892
datum

North race

WEST ELEVATION: medieval masonry

1985 surface

datum   projected window   North race   window   datum

CROSS SECTION A·B

South race

modern roof

buttress bonds
with wall

medieval floor

17th
century
window

medieval floor

■ c1130·46
▨ c1150
□ 13th century
■ concrete

datum

SOUTH ELEVATION: medieval masonry

corbel   corbel

steps

1985 surface   datum

metres
0 1 2 3 4 5   10

86 *The surviving medieval masonry of the Fountains
Abbey mill, with post-medieval additions removed for clarity*

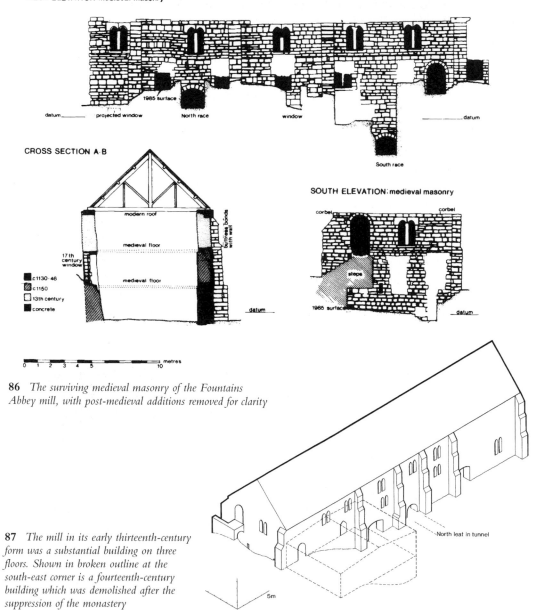

North leat in tunnel

5m

87 *The mill in its early thirteenth-century
form was a substantial building on three
floors. Shown in broken outline at the
south-east corner is a fourteenth-century
building which was demolished after the
suppression of the monastery*

easily controlled. The new mill had two wheels, one at each end, and it had rounded-headed doors and windows. None of the windows survived, for they were converted to two-light windows in the thirteenth century, one jamb only being retained. In the early thirteenth century, the mill was extended to the north and an upper granary floor was added. Further granary space was created in the fourteenth century by adding a wing to the south-east corner of the building (**87**). The mill survived the suppression and continued to work up to 1937, some eight centuries after it was first built; its architecture reflects all the major periods of the abbey's development, and its longevity indicates the quality of its construction. Although devoid of any decoration, the mill is architecturally distinguished, a certain pointer to its importance.

No less important was the woolhouse, a great aisled storehouse of four bays, now reduced almost totally to low walling. Excavation has proved it to be a complex structure, part of a massive range of buildings that included the bake house and brew house, with six principal phases of construction from its first building in the 1150s to its eventual demolition at the end of the fifteenth century (**88**). Essentially, the woolhouse was a great barn with an office for the obedientiary attached to its north-east corner. As the abbey's economy developed throughout the thirteenth century it was enlarged, and by the end of the century it had acquired a fulling mill in its western aisle powered by an undershot wheel. The bake house and brew house to the south were also rebuilt in the late thirteenth century. The fourteenth century saw changes in the use of the complex with the insertion of dye vats in the remains of the fulling mill and the provision of two furnaces to provide hot water. The western aisles were partitioned off and appear to have been used for finishing cloth. No longer was this the woolhouse but a multi-purpose structure. Its final use came in the late fifteenth century when it was partitioned up as

88 *The woolhouse as excavated was a complicated structure with five identifiable periods of building*

123

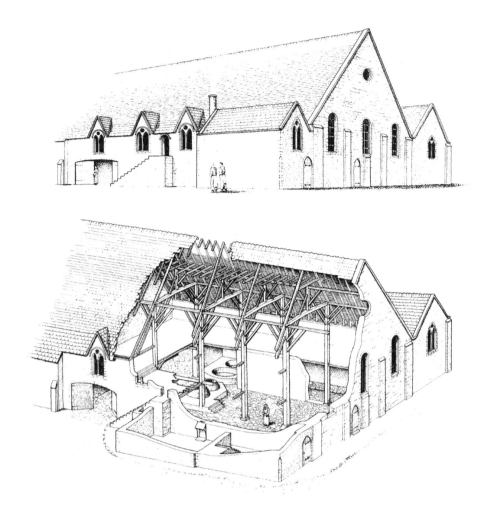

89 *The woolhouse as it would have appeared in the fifteenth century, seen from the north east and reconstructed from the evidence of fallen architectural detail.* Simon Hayfield

workshops used for a restoration of the abbey church. Debris indicated that glaziers were working in the central part of the building, while a small blacksmith's forge was created in the eastern aisle, the smith's tongs and the lead linings of his cooling troughs still lying in the hammer scale on the floor. To the south of the smithy was a pit full of bronze-working debris. The building seems to have been in poor repair by the late fifteenth century, and when it had outlived its usefulness it was demolished, leaving on the south wall which was the north wall of the bake house and brew house. Its site was simply levelled and only reusable walling stone removed. Almost all the architectural detail was thrown down close to its original location, permitting an accurate reconstruction of the building to be made (**89**). Like the mill it was a distinguished building, reflecting the importance of its original use.

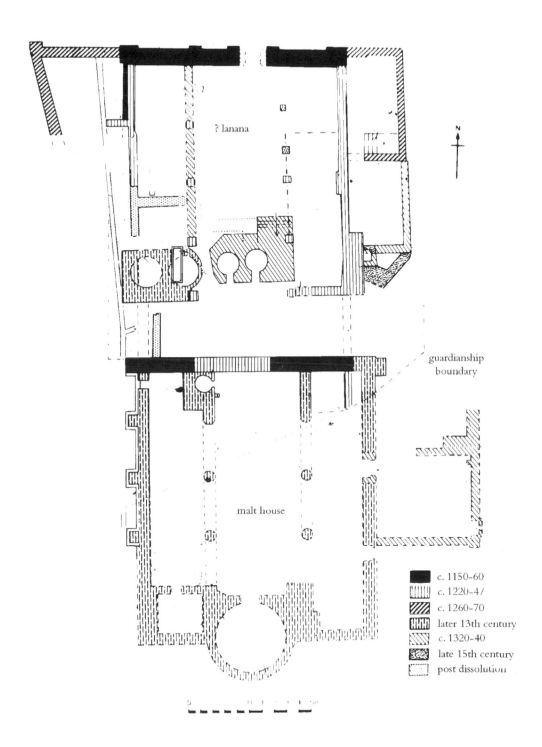

? lanana

guardianship
boundary

malt house

■ c. 1150–60

c. 1220–4/

c. 1260–70

later 13th century

c. 1320–40

late 15th century

post dissolution

90 *The woolhouse (to the north) and bake house and brew house (to the south) together comprised a substantial building under a single roof*

The bake house and brew house, which formed the southern continuation of the woolhouse from the early thirteenth century, was rebuilt in fine ashlar in the 1290s, and with the exception of the addition of an obedientiary's office on its east side in the fourteenth century remained largely unaltered into the sixteenth century (**90**). On two storeys and with three aisles at ground level, it was a substantial building. The ground floor was the bake house, with its great brick-lined bread oven at its south end, and the moulding boards and flour hutches in the aisles; it was last excavated in the 1880s. Re-excavation would identify its use more precisely, but its plan is typical of a monastic bake house. The upper floor is thought to be the brew house for two reasons. First, bake houses and brew houses are always found close together, often in the same building, and second because the upper floor had a piped water supply necessary for brewing but not for most other industrial processes.

Because Fountains lay at the centre of a web of estates and all its granges were focused on the abbey, the outer court was the centre of all the economic activity that supported the monastery. If the cloister buildings were workshops of prayer, the buildings of the outer court were workshops of Mammon, without which the former could not have functioned. It is perhaps symbolic that the cloister buildings have survived so completely when only a handful of grange buildings, and those mainly chapels, survive above ground, and of the outer court buildings only the valuable mill survived demolition in the sixteenth century. The means have been lost but the end survives in recognisable form.

6

FOUNTAINS ABBEY
SINCE THE SUPPRESSION

The end of Fountains as a working abbey came within the general suppression of English monasteries on 26 November 1539. Suppression was inevitable when the government realized that it could take over the lands and wealth of monastic houses. These had become state property when Henry VIII made himself 'Supreme Head (below God) of the church in England' in 1534, though this had been effective since 1531 when Convocation had acknowledged the king as Supreme Head 'so far as the law of Christ allowed'. The beginning of the end came about because of events at Rievaulx in 1533.

The deposing of Abbot William Thirsk

Abbot Edward Kirby of Rievaulx was a conservative abbot who was unlikely to agree with the rapid changes that were occurring in the church in the early 1530s and who fell foul of the patron of his house, Sir Thomas Manners, a staunch supporter of the King's party who was supported by Thomas Cromwell, the King's secretary. Manners sought to depose Abbot Kirby and replace him with a more sympathetic abbot who would understand the needs of both King and Church in changing times. Accordingly, Manners brought an accusation of mismanagement of the abbey's assets against Kirby, who was to be examined by his peers who included the abbots of Fountains and Byland. William Thirsk of Fountains could find no fault with Kirby, presumably because the charges were not true, and though it did not stop Kirby's deposition on Cromwell's authority, William Thirsk was a marked man.

In 1535, Thomas Cromwell was instructed to make a general visitation of all monasteries, both to ascertain their wealth and to enquire into the quality of monastic life. The former exercise produced a detailed assessment of taxable income, the *Valor Ecclesiasticus,* which established that rich pickings were to be had if the monasteries were to be dissolved, and led to the Act of Suppression of 1536 by which all monasteries with an annual income of less than £200 were to be closed down for the benefit of the Crown. Greater monasteries where 'religion was well kept' were to remain. The second survey, conducted in the north by Drs Richard Leyton and Thomas Leigh, unscrupulous individuals chosen more for their loyalty to Cromwell than their desire to reform monastic life, was to examine the morals of the enclosed. They arrived in Yorkshire in January 1536 and having made short work of St Mary's Abbey at York proceeded to Fountains where they started about Abbot Thirsk.

Within the abbey was a monk called Marmaduke Bradley, a schemer who had been in disgrace in the time of the reforming Abbot Huby but who had acquired a pardon for his crimes from Abbot Guillaume du Boisset of Cîteaux. He had inherited a valuable prebendal stall in Ripon Minster, and was seeking to advance his position both within the monastery and outside. Before Leyton and Leigh had visited, Bradley had offered Cromwell 600 marks in hard cash for the abbacy (in addition to the £1000 he would pay to the King over three years for the 'first fruits' due from his appointment). It is hardly surprising that the visitors found severe fault with Abbot Thirsk. Writing to Cromwell on 20 January, Richard Leyton described Thirsk as 'a very fool and a miserable idiot' while Bradley was 'the wisest monk within England of that order and well learned, twenty years officer and ruler of all that house, a wealthy fellow'. There is evidence that Thirsk was not a prudent ruler, for he had been selling the abbey's timber without the convent's agreement, but the visitors went on to accuse him of stealing jewels from the abbey's treasury at dead of night in order to sell them, considerably under-valued, to a Cheapside goldsmith, and of keeping six whores for his own amusement. There is not the slightest evidence to substantiate these allegations, and his only crime was to be a powerful and influential conservative like Abbot Kirby at Rievaulx, but Thirsk was persuaded to resign and make way for Marmaduke Bradley. Given a generous pension (that Bradley tried to have reduced), he retired to live with his friend Adam Sedbar the Abbot of Jervaulx until both men unwisely became involved with the Pilgrimage of Grace and were accordingly butchered at Tyburn.

Leyton and Leigh believed that Marmaduke Bradley, as well as being generous to their master and themselves, would be more politic and pliant than his predecessor, and would better serve the King's interest. In this they were as incorrect as they had been in their reports on Thirsk. Abbot Bradley was going to get the best deal he could for himself and his community.

The suppression of Fountains

Following the northern rising generally known as the Pilgrimage of Grace, that sought amongst other things to restore the lesser monasteries suppressed in 1536, the wealthy and powerful abbeys were plainly at risk. Bridlington and Jervaulx were seized by the King because their superiors had been involved with the rebels and had been tried and executed as traitors. They provided great wealth to the Crown and it was only a short time before the decision was taken to suppress all the remaining houses. A visitation of the greater houses beginning in January 1538 was undertaken with the intention of encouraging their 'voluntary' surrender to the King. This was a long and slow business, extending into 1540, and the turn of Fountains came in November 1539.

Abbot Bradley, his prior Thomas Kydde and 30 monks signed the deed of surrender in the chapter-house on 26 November, ending almost 408 years of uninterrupted monastic life. Bradley succeeded in having his 'first fruits' substantially reduced as he had been unable to enjoy the income of his office as he had intended, and though he had offered to give up his prebend at Ripon on his election he had somehow managed to retain it, and was to keep it until his death in 1553. He also persuaded the suppression commissioners to provide him with an annual pension of £100. His prior was to receive £8, and the monks between £6 13s 4d (£6.66) and £5, fairly standard rates for those who were prepared to go without a fuss. The rewards to the crown were spectacular, and the commissioners could afford to be generous. The abbey's estates provided a clear revenue of more than £1100 a year and the contents of the treasury and sacristies were substantial. A list made before the suppression by Brian Higden, Dean of York, and Edward Kirby of Rievaulx mentions 80 copes amongst other vestments, some of cloth of gold or silver, two mitres encrusted with silver gilt decoration, two croziers with silver heads, no fewer than 22 silver chalices, rich reliquaries of St Anne, St Lawrence and the True Cross, and plate weighing at least 80,51gm. Additionally, the bells and all the lead from the roofs were of considerable value.

The abbey buildings were not immediately dismantled as was the norm, because Henry VIII had devised a scheme to create a new bishopric with jurisdiction over Richmondshire and parts of Lancashire. As a result the buildings were mothballed for a short period before the scheme was abandoned. This short-lived stay of execution might have kept the buildings intact but it did not mean that no damage was done. Excavation by Walbran in the 1850s indicated that many graves had been looted, although he was unable to ascertain when this had happened. The excavation in 1979 of the grave in the south transept of brother John Ripon (**91**) who died in 1524 identified graphically the sequence of events which must have happened while the church was still in royal hands. The grave slab had been lifted and broken, and the upper half of the grave cut dug out, disturbing the body, which was still at least partially articulated, to retrieve the mortuary chalice and paten that had been buried with the priest. The remains of John Ripon were then thrown back into the grave with no attempt to replace them correctly and the grave refilled. This in itself is hardly remarkable, but the next occurrence is. The grave slab was carefully relaid, though part of it had been thrown into the grave fill, and missing areas were made up with plaster, which was not apparent until excavation. Such a restoration can only have taken place within the context of the church being in the care of the suppression commissioners and would imply that the looting, for once at least, was unauthorized.

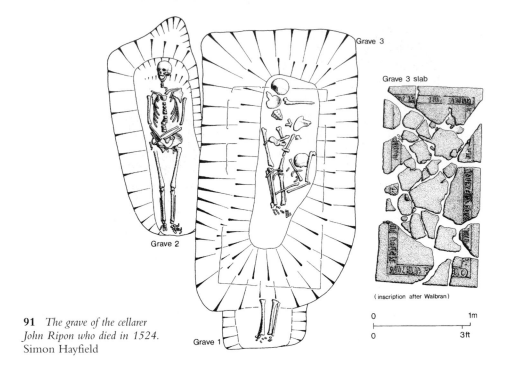

Grave 3

Grave 3 slab

Grave 2

(inscription after Walbran)

91 *The grave of the cellarer John Ripon who died in 1524.* Simon Hayfield

Grave 1

0   1m

0   3ft

The sale of the site

The King's proposal was to come to nothing, and the new diocese was given to Chester Abbey, thus preserving the remains of the Benedictine house there. Before the decision was taken to do this, Cromwell had been in negotiations with Sir Richard Gresham to sell the abbey and its home estates, and the sale was duly completed in October 1540. The dismantling of the abbey now began, for by then window glass and lead from the stripping of Fountains were appearing in Ripon and York. Normally the lead and bells were reserved for the Crown, and Gresham accounted for the casting down and removal of lead as late as 1544, when it was being transported to Hull by way of Boroughbridge and York. Furnaces were built within the abbey church, including one in the crossing, and timber from the roofs and screens used to burn the lead and cast it into sows of approximately half a ton (**92**) for ease of shipment. Not all the lead was destined to reach the King's officials, however, and in 1544, Gresham's receiver John Hall had paid Leonard Beckwith, receiver of the Court of Augmentations which handled the receipts of former monastic estates, the sum of 8d (3p) for making an indictment against 'him that stole the leade at ffountance'.

The scale of Gresham's spoliation is difficult to ascertain, but he seems mainly to have been responsible for the unroofing of the buildings and the recovery of the King's lead, a similar exercise to that carried out by Thomas

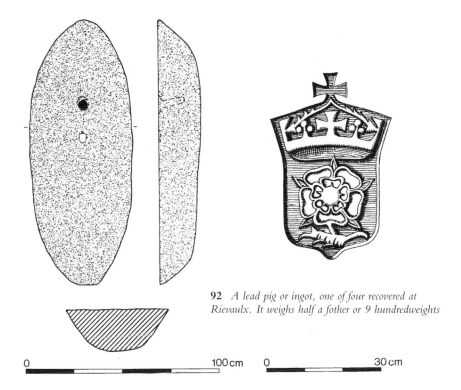

92 *A lead pig or ingot, one of four recovered at Rievaulx. It weighs half a fother or 9 hundredweights*

0   100 cm   0   30 cm

Manners at Rievaulx in 1539. There is also the possibility that it was Gresham's agents who were responsible for the partial demolition of the upper levels of the presbytery and Nine Altars, for all the decorative wall-shafts were ripped out to recover their lead packing-pieces, and the tie-rods that retained the open arcade in front of the clerestory windows were cut, ensuring that the upper works of the building collapsed fairly quickly, making the church unrestorable as the conditions of sale usually required.

The site that Gresham purchased was suitably surveyed before the sale in September 1540 by Leonard Beckwith and Hugh Fuller, and besides the church and cloister buildings, only two buildings were recorded as roofed, the corn mill that still survives and the tannery, both valuable buildings in their own right, though the tannery had been stripped of its contents. The other buildings of the inner and outer courts may already have been demolished for their materials as surplus to requirements, even if the church were to become a cathedral, but only excavation will demonstrate this. Because Gresham had bought the site and its home estates for investment, he had no interest in building himself or his tenant a house out of the ruins, and Fountains was spared the destruction that resulted on so many other monastic sites. It is largely because he only carried out the work he was required to do that Fountains remains one of the most complete Cistercian monasteries of the medieval period.

The building of Fountains Hall

The abbey buildings and part of the home estates were sold by Gresham's son, Sir Thomas, to Stephen Proctor, son of Thomas Proctor, an early ironmaster, in 1597. Knighted in 1604 he acquired the lucrative post of Collector of Fines on Penal Statutes in 1606, and generally annoyed his neighbours by engaging them in endless lawsuits over land and mineral rights and by his relentless persecution of Catholics after the Gunpowder Plot of November 1605, the only zealous Protestant squire in a generally Catholic area. He built himself a small house, Fountains Hall, on the north side of the abbey precinct between the outer and inner gatehouses traditionally in or about 1611, but it must have been substantially complete by 1604 when the infant Prince Charles (later Charles I) and his retinue stayed there. The house (**93**) is a variant on Robert Smythson's design for Woolaton, and it is likely that Smythson provided designs, though he certainly did not oversee the building. Stylistic links can be made with other Smythson houses, notably Chastleton, Pontefract and Hardwick. It is a house of a single, tall façade, terraced into the valley side to increase its dramatic effect. Five storeys high and framed by square battlemented turrets, it is a strangely old-fashioned house hiding behind a fine renaissance front. The hall occupied the ground floor above a basement, with the Great Chamber above, its windows filled with armorial glass by Dinninghof reflecting Proctor's pretensions to gentility.

The house had cost Proctor some £3000 to build although he had been able to take stone from the abbey ruins. Perhaps it was his Protestant distaste for Rome that stopped him taking the best stone of the church and cloister buildings. Instead, he took stone from the abbot's house and infirmary and they owe their generally ruined state to his depredations. Infirmary stone, including a thirteenth-century string-course, can be identified in the east wall of the

93 *The south front of Fountains Hall with its wealth of renaissance detail hides what is essentially a rather old-fashioned house*

house, and the arches over the entrance stairs are medieval and looted from somewhere in the abbey. More remarkably, the spiral stair from the south–west angle of the Nine Altars was removed almost totally, to be re-erected on the west side of the house. However, the greater part of the stone used appears to have been new-quarried, reducing the destruction of the medieval ruins that must have been an uncomfortable reminder of the country's Catholic past.

Sir Stephen Proctor died without an heir in 1619 and the abbey passed through a number of hands until it came into the possession of the Messenger family in the mid-seventeenth century. It was during their ownership that the historian Robert Thoresby visited the ruins in 1682 and described them as 'a noble wreck in ruinous perfection. . . full of trees in the very body of it'. Though they were Catholics, the Messengers appear to have done little to repair the ruins, but equally they did nothing to destroy them, and Fountains was reasonably safe in their hands until it was sold in 1767 to the owner of the adjoining estate of Studley Royal.

The clearance of the abbey ruins in the mid-nineteenth century brought to light some evidence of Civil War activity at Fountains. When the drain of the monks' latrine block was cleared out, a hoard of 354 silver pennies was found buried in the silt below the arch that carried the east wall of the abbot's chamber over the drain. These coins ranged in date from the reign of Mary Tudor up to the reign of Charles I, and had been placed where they might easily have been recovered. Presumably whoever placed these coins there was unable to return and recover them. More graphic evidence was recovered when the walls that blocked off both ends of the sacristy on the south side of the south transept were removed to reveal 'a mass of human bones, sufficient according to a careful computation, to have formed not less than 400 skeletons' At the time they were thought to have been bodies disturbed by the looting of medieval graves but recent excavation has shown that monastic burials that were disturbed were simply left lying about the site. More likely, such a cache represents the dead of a local Civil War action.

John Aislabie, the South Sea Bubble, and the gardens of Studley Royal

To the east of Fountains in the Middle Ages was the village of Studley. By the third quarter of the seventeenth century it had long been deserted and was in the possession of George Aislabie, Registrar of the Ecclesiastical Court at York, as the inheritance of his wife Mary, the eldest daughter of Sir John Mallory. Their son, John Aislabie, inherited the Studley estate on his mother's death in 1699. Socially and politically ambitious, he was the Tory MP for Ripon, though he was to turn his coat and join the Whigs, becoming Chancellor of the Exchequer in 1718.

94 *The remodelled valley of the River Skell seen from Aislabie's 'rustic bridge'*

In 1711, the South Sea Company was formed to trade with the Spanish Americas, a trade which was mistakenly thought to be highly profitable. Speculation was rife, with many unscrupulous speculators obtaining subscriptions from the public to invest in the company. Shares rose dramatically in value and Aislabie was one of the sponsors of an Act of Parliament enabling people owed money by the state to convert their claims into South Sea shares. The share price rose from £100 to £1000 and then collapsed in 1720 when the cashier Mr Knight absconded with £100,000, causing widespread ruin. Disgraced, John Aislabie was expelled from Parliament and disqualified from holding public office for life. Wealthy but embittered, he returned to Yorkshire where he directed his considerable energies into the creation of a formal pleasure garden on his Studley Royal estate.

Work had actually begun on the garden in 1716 but the first phase, the creation of a new landscape, was not completed until 1730. The Skell valley was drastically remodelled with the river itself diverted into a canal at the centre of the valley with geometric ponds formed to either side (**94**). At the western boundary of the estate, where the canal joined the unimproved Skell, a half-moon pond was created to act as a reservoir and Tent Hill, a conical mound, created to provide a vista. At the east end of the canal a new lake was created in Studley Park, the junction marked by a cascade. The scale of the earthmoving was tremendous, with about 100 men employed seasonally under the direction of John Simpson. Additionally, seven contractors were employed to bring stone 6.4km from Galphay Moor. The garden was designed by

95   *The Temple of Piety seen across Aislabie's canal, the circular Moon Pond and the Crescent Ponds*

Aislabie himself, heavily influenced by the great French formal gardener le Nôtre and by Queen Anne's gardeners, George London and Henry Wise.

The garden buildings, all originally severely classical, were later additions to the design (**95**), and were built after 1732. Over 10 years, two temples, an orangery (**96**), the Octagon Tower, and various bridges were built. By Aislabie's death in 1742, the garden was largely complete. It formed a contrast with the abbey ruins that remained a vista at the west end of the gardens. Aislabie had originally intended to buy the Fountains estate from the Messengers and a price of £4000 had been agreed when he suddenly wthdrew.

96   *The Orangery, later refitted as a banqueting house, was probably designed by Colen Cambell and built between 1728 and 1732*

97 *Aislabie's vista of Fountains Abbey was painted by Balthazar Nebot in about 1760, a free view of the ruin he failed to acquire.* National Trust

98 *Aislabie's vista of Ripon Minster along the great avenue in Studley Royal Park, also painted by Nebot, indicates the close connection between the genteel classical design of the gardens and the rude gothic of a monumental building in the landscape that was too good to ignore.* National Trust

Perhaps he agreed with the traveller Arthur Young who concluded that 'ruins generally appear best at a distance'. In any case, he had his vista. Indeed, the focus of Aislabie's most dramatic avenue along the drive from Studley to Ripon was the minster church there, and it is instructive that so formal a landscape should have such imposing views of gothic buildings that contrasted so strongly with the classical design of his own buildings (**97** & **98**).

William Aislabie and Fountains Abbey

John Aislabie's son William inherited the Studley Royal estate on his father's death in 1742, when the main work on the garden was complete. His contribution was to continue the landscaping of the lower Skell valley towards Ripon and to buy the Fountains estate in 1768 for the immense sum of £16,000. Tastes had changed since John Aislabie had designed his garden, and William broke away from formality to follow the picturesque approach which was to become the hallmark of Lancelot 'Capability' Brown in the last quarter of the eighteenth century. Fountains was no longer to be a vista but the ruins were brought into the garden itself, set in an informal sweep of lawns and framed with trees (**99**).

The ruins were not quite to William Aislabie's taste, so they were improved, not simply by selective demolition, but by the addition of new features. Gilpin, who visited in 1772 was not at all impressed by Aislabie's treatment of the abbey:

> A few fragments scattered about the body of a ruin are proper and picturesque. They are proper because they account for what is defaced; and they are picturesque, because they unite the principal parts with the round in which union the beauty of composition in good measure depends. But here they are thought rough and unsightly and fell a sacrifice to neatness .... In the room of these detached parts, which are proper and picturesque embellishments of the scene, a gaudy temple is erected, and other trumpery wholly foreign to it. But not only is the scene defaced, and the *outworks of the ruin* violently torn away; *the main body of the ruin itself* is at this very time under the alarming hand of decoration. When the present proprietor made his purchase, he found the whole mass of ruins – the Cloisters, the Abbey Church, and the Hall – choked with rubbish. The first work therefore was to clear and open. And something in this might have been done with propriety, for we see ruins so choked that no view of them can be obtained ....But the restoration of parts is not enough: ornament must be added [**100**], and such incongruous ornament, as disgrace the scene are disgracing also the monastery. The monks' garden is turned into a trim parterre and planted with flowering shrubs; a view is opened up through the great window to some ridiculous I know not what (Anne Bolein I think they call it) that is planted in the valley; and in the central part of the abbey, a circular pedestal is raised out fragments of the old pavement, on which is erected a mutilated heathen statue!

While Gilpin's complaints were largely a matter of taste, it is obvious that Aislabie did considerable damage to the archaeology and structure of the site. He swept away the remains of the elegant late twelfth-century cloister arcades, the tracery of the major windows of the church, and the arcades of the presbytery and the enclosing screen of the high altar. He also reduced the ground level there, destroying John of Kent's mosaic tile pavement. Elsewhere, he spread fallen masonry around the site to establish new levels for his all-pervasive lawns, removing architectural detail from its original context and burying the bases of the nave piers and the shattered ruins of the abbot's house and infirmary. We are fortunate that antiquaries had already begun to show an interest in the ruins, and Thomas Greaves had drawn a detailed plan of what was visible before Aislabie began his 'improvements'. There was of course a positive side to Aislabie's acquisition of the ruins. As they were meant to adorn his landscape they had to be made secure and for the first time since 1539 they were repaired and maintained, ensuring their long-term survival. The architectural detail from the buildings he destroyed was spread about the site to be recovered in more recent times when it was appreciated for the information it retained.

On William Aislabie's death in 1781 his estate passed to his daughter, Mrs Allanson, who was persuaded by the antiquary John Martin of Ripon to allow the excavation of the chapter-house. Martin had read Burton's *Monasticon Eboracense* which contained a transcript of the abbey's 'President Book' and believed he would find the graves of important abbots there. The estate gardener was commissioned to dig the room out in 1790-1, and indeed the graves of the presidents from Richard of Clairvaulx to William Rigton were revealed. In the course of this excavation, one of the earliest on any monastic site, the method of

99 *The ruins of Fountains abbey in the informal landscape of the late eighteenth century*

100 *William Aislabie constructed a 'shrine' below the east window of the Nine Altars, recorded before it was removed by Walbran in the 1850s*

destruction of the chapter-house was revealed. The monolithic marble piers had been cut to take wedges that had been driven in to crack the stone, ropes were then attached to the piers, and horses or oxen used to pull the columns out allowing the vault to fall. Precisely the same technique was noted in the chapter-house at Rievaulx when it was excavated in the early 1920s. The excavation of 1790 recovered the greater part of the vault, which was simply carted out into the cloister where it remained until 1851, obscuring the chapter-house façade.

Fountains Abbey in the nineteenth century

In 1808, Mrs Allanson's niece, Mrs Lawrence, inherited the estate and began a lengthy campaign of repairs. In 1822, the southern part of the vault of the west range fell and was reconstructed. Excavation in 1987 revealed the evidence for shoring put up to support what had survived the fall, showing that great care had been taken to save as much historic fabric as possible. Hardly any new stone was used, and it is only the mortar used which revealed parts of the vault had been reconstructed. The site was first opened to the public in 1824, providing an income to offset the cost of repair.

In 1840, it was found that the transverse arches of the aisle vaults in the church were in need of repair before they too fell, particularly in the south nave aisle. Here some were taken down and rebuilt, the stones being marked with Roman numerals to ensure they were replaced in the correct order. To do this work, scaffolding was required and holes to secure this were dug in the uneven surface of Aislabie's dumped material. Richard Walbran, an antiquarian and archaeologist from Ripon, was quick to see the potential revealed by these excavations:

> In clearing away, at that time, the mounds of rubbish that had accu-
> mulated in the southern aisle, the great square base of one of the

columns of the nave was accidentally exposed; and on following it down to the floor, a singular and early geometrical painted pavement, apparently the floor of a chapel, was observed near the door leading to the Cloister Court. A few more openings were afterwards made, almost at random, in different parts of the church.

So began the serious archaeological study of the site under Walbran's direction. The workmen found a large gravestone (**62**) between the eastern crossing piers, believed at the time to be that of Abbot John of Ripon (but now known to be that of Thomas Swinton), and lifted it to reveal 'the perfect skeleton of a very tall man … resting on a paved bed immediately below the stone; but no trace of a ring, chalice, paten, or any other relic or substance whatever was observed'. Mrs Lawrence, a devout Anglican, was appalled by this sacrilege and Walbran's work was abruptly terminated in 1841.

Mrs Lawrence died in 1845, and in the following year the Royal Archaeological Institute, holding its summer meeting in Leeds, visited the abbey with Walbran as their guide. He outlined his previous work and made the case for the continued excavation of the site. The Earl de Grey, the new owner of the site and President of the Royal Institute of British Architects, did not immediately rise to the challenge, though he did continue the programme of repair. In 1848 he began repairs to the tunnels that had carried John of Kent's infirmary over the River Skell, and following the discovery of a tile floor Walbran was invited to undertake an excavation from November of that year. This was carried out with a remarkable attention to detail that marks Walbran as one of the first modern archaeologists.

Walbran mistook the building he was excavating for the abbot's house, an easy mistake to make at the time when the buildings of any monastery were not fully understood, and his error has coloured his interpretation but not invalidated his work. His observations were remarkably acute for the mid-nineteenth century and his approach was strangely modern: 'as the ground plan may be easily defined, and important fragments of the superstructure were found within the area, a tolerably accurate idea of its former appearance can be obtained.' The masonry he recovered was carefully stacked to the south west of the infirmary hall where it remained until 1988, and it can be studied in the context of Walbran's published description of the excavation. It was Walbran who discovered that the infirmary hall had been subdivided from the late fourteenth century, and that 'Tudor' windows had been inserted to light the new apartments. His attention to detail is even more apparent when he was dealing with non-structural evidence. Between the misericord and the infirmary passage he found a yard where 'the last supply of coal that the house had needed remained under the sward', below which was a thick deposit of domestic rubbish, treasure trove to an archaeologist. Here:

there was a silver spoon, weighing about an ounce, with a capacious bowl, slender octagonal stem, and a head similar to an inverted Tudor bracket. Then broken pottery ware that had disappeared from the abbot's table, to the large coarse home-made jugs that after a 'mere crack' had been broken in the kitchen; a small silver ornament in the shape of a lion's face, apparently detached from a larger object; a silver ring; a broad brass ring; a copper can; a sickle blade; several Nuremberg tokens; part of a small ornament in lead, resembling the tracery of a Tudor window, and proving the application of architectural forms to domestic utensils; a quantity of beef, mutton, pork and venison bones, together with those of poultry, herons, and other game; with bushels of oyster, mussel, and cockle shells, as fresh and pearly as when they left abbot Bradley's table.

This was the waste from the misericord, testimony to the diet and possessions of late Cistercian monks. Walbran found in these items the close connection with people who were already so well known to him from a lifetime's study of the abbey's documents, and so it was that he recorded them so lovingly, to the extent that many of the objects can still be identified today. By the spring of 1850 the whole of the infirmary was exposed, and some of its fallen masonry reset for display (**101**).

The 1850 season saw Walbran's attention turn to the ruins of the real abbot's house and the monks' latrine, buried to a depth of 2m below raised parterres and which were only partly known from Greave's plan. In the process of excavating the prison cells below the abbot's hall he encountered the latrine drain

101 *Walbran reset two piers in the infirmary that he had found in a fallen state*

102 *The site following Walbran's excavation was stripped of fallen material and had largely taken on its present appearance*

of Murdac's monastery where 'the stench was so intolerable as to require quicklime to be thrown in before it could be cleaned out', sadly destroying any environmental evidence that had survived there from the 1140s and 50s.

Walbran had now revealed parts of the monastery lost to view since the seventeenth century and had established with de Grey a new approach to laying out the abbey ruins, no longer in the romantic fashion of the late eighteenth century but to suit the more precise taste of the mid-nineteenth century with its scholarly approach to medieval architecture (**102**). The treatment was thus established for the rest of the site, changing the ruins from an object of curiosity to a stripped exposition of medieval architecture without the evidence of decay.

Walbran turned his attention once more to the church in 1851, beginning at the south end of the Nine Altars and working westwards, an operation which required the installation of a light railway that ran out of the west door of the nave and which was not completed until late in 1853. His objective was to clear the church to floor level and recover the evidence of floors, graves, and missing structural parts. In this he was only partially successful, for Aislabie had removed the floors and arcades of the presbytery, and his workmen did not have the skills of present day archaeologists. In the Nine Altars he failed to find the grave of Abbot Gower, but a burial was discovered lying north to south above floor level where Gower was known to be buried. Walbran thought it might be someone buried after the abbey was suppressed, but failed to see that it was probably Gower's embalmed body that had been thrown out of his grave when it was looted in the sixteenth century. It was not until he reached the crossing that he began to find what he was looking for. First to be revealed was the ledger of Abbot Swinton which he had first seen in 1840. Next came the transepts where floors survived and he discovered the slab of brother John Ripon in the south transept and an unmarked slab in the south-west corner of the north transept, perhaps covering the burial of Abbot Huby robbed of its superstructure. In the south transept, his workmen emptied a robbed grave in front of the northern chapel, exposing as they went masonry of the first stone church that Walbran failed to recognise or even record. In the southern chapel he found quantities of masons' chippings, evidence of stone being reworked there after the suppression. The southern chapel had been cleared out in 1849 when its vault was repaired and was found to retain small areas of its mosaic tile pavement from the early thirteenth century. In the crossing, the accidental sinking of a wheelbarrow wheel revealed the presence of the acoustic pits beneath the choir stalls, but of the grave slabs of the abbots buried there, there was no trace. By the excavation of the nave 'little information was obtained' though up to 1.3m of debris was removed to reveal the bases of the piers. At the west end, however, 'two blocks of limestone, each two feet three inches square, with a circle inscribed on the surface, were found inserted into the floor, which led to a more particular examination, ending in the discovery of fifty of similar character'. These were processional markers of Huby's time. Next the galilee porch was cleared and part of its fallen arcade reassembled, the remainder being dumped in the east guest house where it remained until 1985. Among the fallen debris that buried the porch was Darnton's statue of the Virgin and Child which was reset in its niche above the west window, completing the clearance of the church.

Walbran also cleared the main cloister ranges, removing the worst of Aislabie's 'heathen' decorations. A crab-apple press was brought from the west range and set on an old foundation at the centre of the cloister garth, and architectural fragments were laid out on the tops of low walls for display. Sadly, Walbran did not live to write a full account of his work. While working on a definitive study of the abbey's documents he suffered a serious stroke in April 1868 and died twelve months later. It was left to another remarkable man to record the buildings that Walbran had uncovered and brought to the attention of scholars and visitors.

Arthur Reeve was an architectural assistant of William Burges who was engaged on the design and construction of St Mary's Church at Studley Royal for the Marquis and Marchioness of Ripon from 1870. To learn about the detail of medieval architecture, Burges told Reeve that he could do no better than study the buildings of Fountains Abbey. This he did, sponsored by the Marquis, recording not only in plan but also in elevation (**103**) all the visible remains of the abbey. This *tour de force* was undertaken from 1873 to 1876 and

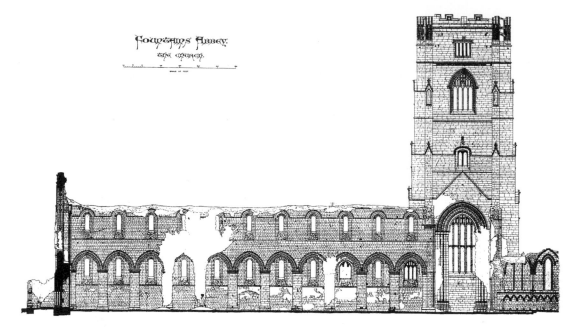

103 *Reeve's drawing of the north side of the nave, crossing, and Huby's tower as it was in 1876*

the exquisite ink and colour wash drawings were kept in the library in Fountains Hall until 1966. They are now owned by English Heritage. Reeve began his work on the west range, where by his own admission he did not record every stone as he found it. However, by the time he had moved on to the guest houses in 1873 he had rectified that failing and his drawings are from then on a true record of what he saw at a scale of 1:96. The most important aspect of Reeve's work was that he drew those parts of the site that Walbran had revealed and which had remained exposed and had not yet suffered any serious deterioration. He may also have done some minor excavation himself to clear partially buried walls, for his plan of the woolhouse (**104**), which he identified as the bake-house, shows walls that Walbran had not investigated but which only survived a few courses high and must have been buried. Reeve did not publish his work until 1892 when he wrote a lengthy text to accompany his drawings and produced a series of reconstruction drawings based on his original record (**103** & **105**). By delaying the publication of his work he was able to collaborate with the most competent monastic archaeologist of the late nineteenth century, Sir William St John Hope.

Hope, the Assistant Secretary of the Society of Antiquaries of London, undertook two seasons of excavation and research at Fountains in September 1887 and 1888 on behalf of the Yorkshire Archaeological Society. His work was basically to follow up points that Walbran had established nearly forty years previously, and to interpret the buildings in the light of his unrivalled

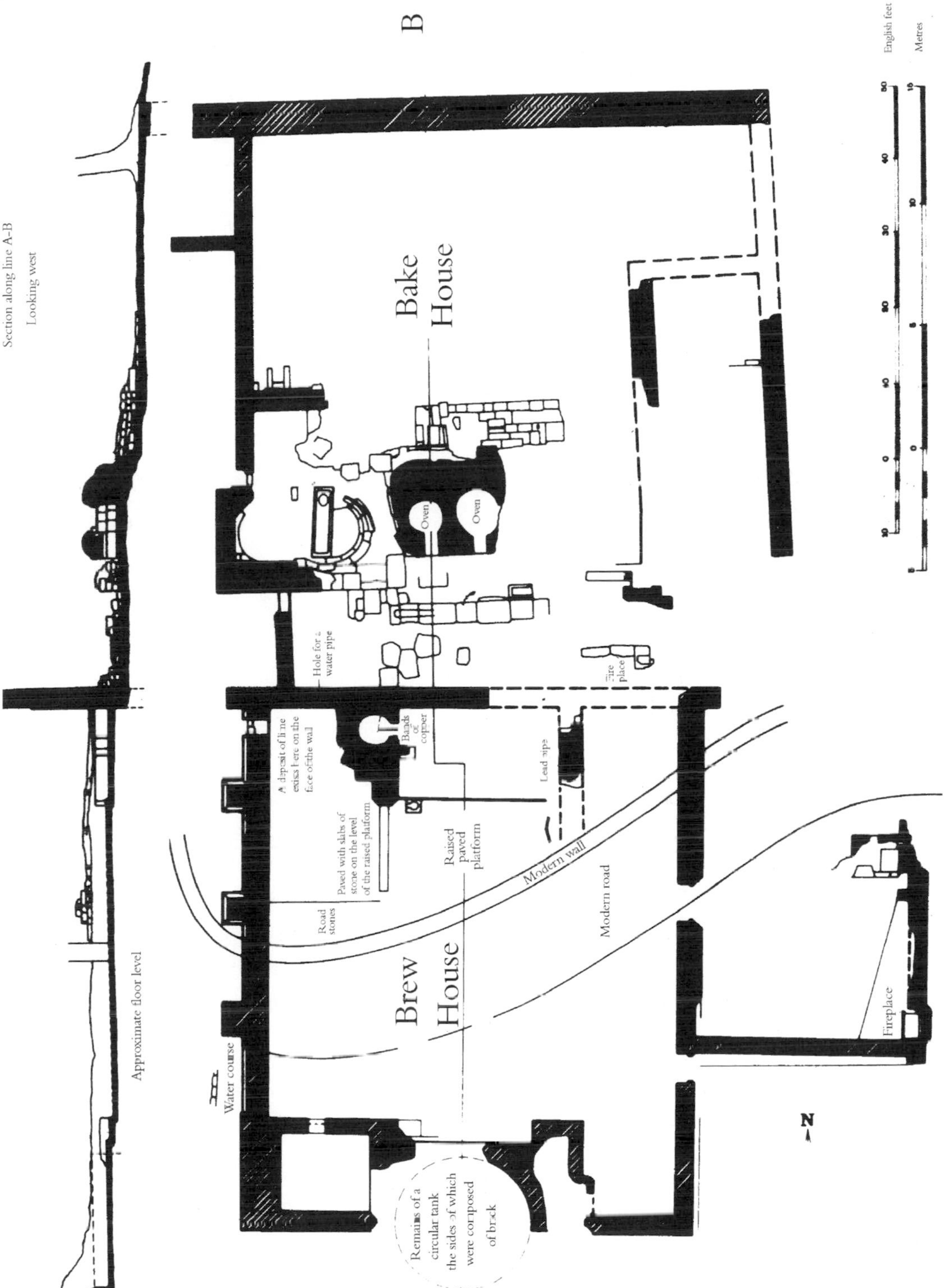

Section along line A-B
Looking west

Approximate floor level

B

Bake House

Oven   Oven

Fire place

Hole for a water pipe

A deposit of lime exists here on the face of the wall

Bands of copper

Lead pipe

Paved with slabs of stone on the level of the raised platform

Raised paved platform

Road stones

Modern wall

Modern road

Brew House

Water course

Remains of a circular tank the sides of which were composed of brick

Fireplace

N

A

English feet

Metres

104 *The 'bake house' and 'brew house', now known to be the wool house and bake house, were recorded after excavation by Reeve*

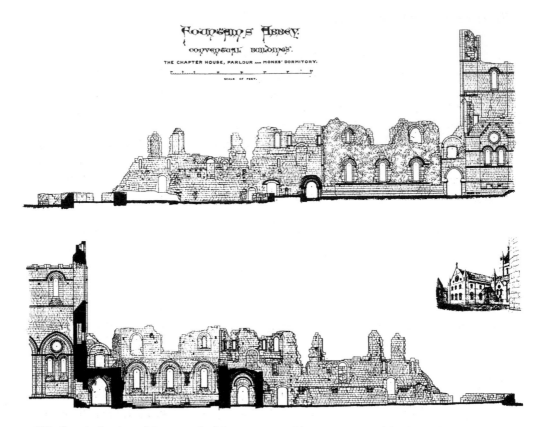

105 *Reeve's elevations of the east wall of the east range and his reconstruction of the chapter-house in its late twelfth-century form*

knowledge of monastic sites. Hope was responsible for the recovery of the plan of the east end of Richard of Clairvaux's church; for resolving the partitioning of the church (**31** & **58**); and for the identification of the pre-1146 fire west, south, and east cloister ranges. His excavation was restricted to strategically placed trenches no more than 0.6m wide that did remarkably little damage to the site's archaeology. It was at Fountains that he first established the general layout of a typical Cistercian monastery, an interpretation which remains valid today. His publication of the site in 1900 set a new standard in the presentation of monastic buildings, comparing the remains of Fountains with the remains of 'nearly all the Cistercian monasteries in this country'. His debt to Reeve and Walbran was great but he was the first person truly to understand the ruins and appreciate their importance both nationally and internationally. He was also instrumental in having the ivy that grew all over the ruins, a pet hate of his wherever he went, removed to conserve the fabric and expose more of it for study. What he did not appreciate was that the ivy actually protected the walls and the painted decoration that remained on them. Most of the evidence for painted decoration has been lost as a result.

Fountains Abbey today

The recent history of Fountains is basically one of repair and presentation to an increasing number of visitors. Although the site had been kept in good repair into the third quarter of the nineteenth century, it was then allowed to deteriorate and by the late 1920s the ruins were in a dangerous state. Although they were privately owned, the Office of Works was sufficiently concerned to undertake a study of the site, make recommendations to the estate regarding the necessary repairs, and offer grant-aid. As a result, the estate began a new campaign of repair, employing a permanent team of stone masons (**106**), which continued up to 1966 when the estate was sold to the West Riding County Council who placed the ruins in the guardianship of the Ministry of Public Buildings and Works. Ownership passed to North Yorkshire County Council after local government reorganisation in 1973 and North Yorkshire in turn sold the Studley Royal Estate to the National Trust in 1983. Today, the ruins are managed by English Heritage, the lineal successor of the old Office of Works.

Being in the guardianship of the state, the abbey ruins have a reasonably assured future, and since 1966 a full programme of conservation and repair has been in progress. This work will not be fully completed until 2010. The conservation of ancient monuments, however, has a down side. Inevitably the evidence of historic fabric is altered as new stone is inserted to replace stone that has failed or been seriously eroded, and as old and decayed mortar pointing is cut out and renewed. Ground disturbance to repair failed foundations or to install power cables and land drains, both necessary for the presentation of the site to an increasingly sophisticated public, is destructive of buried archaeological deposits. Equally, buildings that were meant to have roofs remain at risk from the elements when the roofs are removed, with the loss of once-crisp architectural detail, plaster, and paint from exposed wall surfaces. Consequently, any conscientious

106 *Repair of the parapets of Huby's tower were carried out in the 1930s without the modern requirement for scaffolding*

107 *The excavation of the woolhouse in 1977-80 was the first major archaeological project to be undertaken at Fountains since the mid-nineteenth century and began the recent intensive study of the site*

attempt to maintain the ruins has to be coupled with a recording of the evidence that survives before it is modified or lost. At Fountains this has meant having archaeologists and architectural historians recording the fabric before it is repaired and advising on the least destructive methods of conservation. Without that record this book could not have been written.

Excavation began in 1968 in advance of a scheme to install flood lights to improve the presentation of the monument, a decision taken by the Minister of Public Buildings and Works himself. Trenches 1m deep were dug in all parts of the site, revealing for the first time that there were deep deposits below those recorded by Walbran and Hope. Hope's recording of the mid-twelfth-century east end of the church and of the first phase of the west range was confirmed, and cables were routed so as not to damage buried walls. Unfortunately, the cable trenches did damage buried features, as later excavation was to prove. It is unlikely, however, that there would have been further excavation if the potential of the site had not been demonstrated by the digging of the cable trenches.

It was not until 1977 that large-scale excavation was undertaken, beginning with the site of Reeve and Hope's bake house. There, low walls were exposed for the nineteenth-century excavation trenches had not been backfilled and they needed to be conserved. This could not be done until the building had been re-excavated (**107**) to demonstrate what was medieval and what was not. The result was to prove that considerable amounts of information could be recovered from a building which had been badly disturbed in the nineteenth century, and the building was finally identified as the abbey's woolhouse. From there, attention was turned to the abbey church in 1979 when a problem with drainage was identified. Excavation there recovered the partial plan of two earlier churches, one of timber and one of stone. The stone church had been seen in two small trenches in 1968 but too little was visible to make anything of it. However, by

108 *Open universi-ty students recording a partially blocked window in the east wall of Abbot Murdac's east cloister range.* Keith Emerick

1980 the true significance of the earlier buildings was apparent. There was not one monastery on the site but three, and a detailed examination of the standing buildings and further excavation would reveal with remarkable clarity the way in which the abbey had developed between 1133 and 1170. Excavation in the west range in advance of repairing the tunnels that carried the range over the river revealed the southern end of the 1140s range with a post-fire extension in 1987, and the northern part of the first east range was examined in 1988-9. In both instances it was possible to link below-ground archaeology with standing masonry to reveal how much of the pre-1146 monastery was still standing. Elsewhere, the east guest house was excavated in 1987 in advance of its repair, and in 1990 geophysical survey located the long suspected seven-bay aisled guest hall to the north of the twelfth-century guest houses. The mill, a complex and monumental building, and the only one to survive the suppression of the abbey, was finally repaired between 1998 and 2000.

The detailed recording of upstanding masonry began in the woolhouse in 1978, but it was the study of the mill in 1984, in greater detail than attempted by Reeve and with the intention of analysing its development, that showed the potential for a more general programme of recording. This continued with parts of the surviving precinct wall which was to be repaired and extended to the medieval walls that canalised the Skell within the precinct and the standing cloister buildings (**108**) and church. As well as recording the stonework, the scale drawings produced detailed the evidence of mortars, painted decoration, masons' marks, and scaffolding. When complete, this record will provide the basic information for a full analysis of the ruins and their modification through time, taking the archaeological study of the site from below ground level to the very tops of the walls. Quite simply, Fountains will be the best known and understood medieval monastic site in the world.

FURTHER READING

Because of its exceptional nature, Fountains Abbey is one of the most studied and published monastic sites in Europe and the reader is somewhat spoiled for choice in reading about it. Because a lot has happened on the site since the mid-1970s, however, it is always wise to treat older publications with caution.

For background reading, the best introduction to the Cistercians in northern England is P. J. Fergusson, *The Architecture of Solitude* (Princeton 1984), and for the more general order in Britain, D. Robinson (ed) *The Cistercians in Britain* (B.T. Batsford 1998 & 2002). For the order's earliest buildings in England, see R. Halsey, 'The earliest architecture of the Cistercians in England' in C. Norton & D. Park (eds) *Cistercian Art and Architecture in the British Isles* (Cambridge 1986). This volume contains two other papers, C. Wilson, 'The Cistercians as "missionaries of Gothic" in Northern England' and N. Coldstream, 'Cistercian architecture from Beaulieu to the Dissolution' which provide the background for the later twelfth- and-thirteenth century development of Fountains in its wider context. A general description of the site can be found in four places: G. M. Hills, 'Fountains Abbey, Yorkshire' in *Collectanea Archaeologica* 2 (1871); W. H. St John Hope's 'Fountains Abbey' in *Yorkshire Archaeological Journal* 15 (1900); in A. W. Oxford's *The Ruins of Fountains Abbey* (London 1910); and R. Gilyard-Beer's *Fountains Abbey* (London 1984). These four works record the developing interpretation of the site and demonstrate a largely historical and architectural approach to the ruins.

Particular aspects of the site have been examined in more detail. The timber phase of the monastery has been placed in context by P. J. Fergusson: 'The first architecture of the Cistercians in England and the work of Abbot Adam of Meaux' *Journal of the British Archaeological Association* 136 (1983) and more recently in G. Coppack, C. Hayfield, and R. Williams 'Sawley Abbey: the Architecture and Archaeology of a Smaller Cistercian Abbey' *Journal of the British Archaeological Association* 155 (2002), a paper which also examines the planning of Richard of Clairvaux's new church at Fountains. The first stone monastery was initially discussed by R. Gilyard-Beer in 'Fountains Abbey, the early buildings 1132-50' in *Archaeological Journal* 125 (1968). This paper has been substantially revised by more recent research described in R. Gilyard-Beer and G. Coppack 'Excavations at Fountains Abbey, North Yorkshire, 1979-80: the early development of the monastery' in *Archaeologia* 108 (1986). The excavation of the woolhouse in the outer court is described in G. Coppack 'The excavation of an Outer Court building, perhaps the Woolhouse, at Fountains Abbey, North Yorkshire' in *Medieval Archaeology* 30 (1986). The mill is analysed in G. Coppack 'The water-driven corn mill at Fountains Abbey: a major Cistercian mill of the twelfth and thirteenth centuries' in M. Lillich (ed) *Studies in Cistercian Art and Architecture 5* (Kalamazoo 1998), and the development of the outer court is assessed in G. Coppack 'The Outer Courts of Fountains and Rievaulx Abbeys' in L. Pressouyre (ed) *L'espace cistercien* (Paris 1994). For Richard Walbran's excavations of the mid-nineteenth century, there are summary reports in J. Raine (ed) 'Memorials of Fountains Abbey II', *Surtees Society* 67 (1876). Further accounts of his work can be found in J. R. Walbran's *Guide to Ripon* (1862 and earlier editions). An English translation of the *Narratio de fundatione fontanis monasterii* can be found in Oxford's *Ruins of Fountains Abbey* and in Latin in J. R. Walbran, 'Memorials of Fountains Abbey I', *Surtees Society* 42 (1842).

For the abbey's estates, the basic material is to be found in W. T. Lancaster (ed) 'Abstracts of the Charters and Other Documents Contained in the Chartulary of the Cistercian Abbey of Fountains', 2 vols (Leeds 1915). For granges generally, and Cowton in particular, see C. Platt *The Monastic Grange in Medieval England* (London 1969). For a recent review of the monastic economy in northern England see S. Moorhouse 'Monastic estates, their composition and development' in R. Gilchrist and H. Mytum (eds) 'The Archaeology of Rural Monasteries', *British Archaeological Reports. British Series,* 203 (1989), and J. Roebuck and A. Davison 'Protecting the Cistercian Landscape: a View from North Yorkshire' in L. Pressouyre (ed) *L'espace cistercien* (Paris 1994).

FOUNTAINS ABBEY
AND OTHER SITES TO VISIT

The north of England is particularly rich in the ruins of Cistercian abbeys, of which Fountains is by far the best preserved, though not necessarily the most informative. Taken together, these sites provide a clear picture of the rigorous reformed monasticism that the order introduced into England, its scale, its asceticism, and its wealth. In addition to Fountains there are seven other Cistercian sites which are open to the public. Other sites mentioned in the text lie on private land and can only be visited by prior arrangement.

Fountains Abbey

Fountains Abbey lies 6.4km to the south west of Ripon in North Yorkshie, on the south side of the B6265 to Pateley Bridge. The abbey ruins lie at the west end of the Studley Royal Estate which is owned by the National Trust, and can be visited throughout the year (except for Fridays in November, December and January, Christmas Day and Boxing Day). The abbey ruins are in the guardianship of the Secretary of State for Culture, Media and Sport and are maintained by English Heritage. There is a charge for admission. Visitors have access to the greater part of the abbey ruins and to the water mill which contains an exhibition. The outer court and precinct wall are not generally accessible, lying on tenanted farmland, but the precinct wall can be seen from the road which skirts the western side of the precinct. The only home grange to which there is public access is Swanley, the site of the National Trust's visitor centre. The public can also visit the early seventeenth-century Fountains Hall and the eighteenth-century park and gardens of Studley Royal within which lies the nineteenth-century church of St Mary, Studley Royal, managed by the National Trust on behalf of English Heritage and open daily from 1-5pm from 29 March to 30 September.

Rievaulx Abbey

Fountains' great rival, Rievaulx Abbey, lies 5km west of Helmsley in North Yorkshire to the south of the B1257 to Stokesley. Substantial ruins of the church and cloister buildings remain and are in the care of English Heritage. The site is open all year apart from New Year's Day, Christmas Day and Boxing Day, and there is a charge for admission. The site has a new visitor centre which examines the abbey's economy, explains its complicated buildings, and displays many of the architectural and archaeological finds from its excavation. Rievaulx is a more complex site than Fountains and is more heavily ruined. Its buildings, however, are much more informative because more detail has survived. This is particularly true of the church and dormitory ranges. In addition to the church and cloister ranges, the village church, still in use, incorporates the remains of the gate chapel, and parts of the inner gatehouse remain in the churchyard boundary. The buildings of the inner and outer courts lie under the post-suppression village that clusters to the west of the church and one mill, substantially rebuilt, survives, though it is now a private house. The remainder of the precinct is farmland to which limited access can be gained by public footpath.

Furness Abbey

The third great Cistercian abbey in the North was Furness Abbey, the ruins of which survive 3km north of Barrow in Furness in Cumbria on the east side of the A590. The site is managed by English Heritage and is open all year apart from New Year's Day, Christmas Day, Boxing Day, and Mondays and Tuesdays from 1 November to 31 March. There is a charge for admission. The principal surviving buildings are the church, east range, abbot's house and infirmary, though the whole precinct survives as parkland within an enclosing precinct wall with two surviving gatehouses and a gate chapel. The low walling of the inner gatehouse also survives, and a roofed building, apparently a mill, survives in the southern part of the precinct. This is not open to the public. The visitor centre contains an exhibition on the history and economy of the abbey and a display of an exceptional collection of tomb covers and architectural detail.

Kirkstall Abbey

Fountains' daughter house of Kirkstall lies in public parkland to the north west of Leeds adjacent to the A65 and close to Headingley station. The site is owned and managed by Leeds City Council which maintains a museum in the intact inner gatehouse. Being in parkland, much of the site can be visited at any reasonable time, but until repairs are completed access to the interior of the church and cloister ranges is by appointment only (the buildings are unsafe).

The church and cloister ranges are remarkably well preserved and for the most part contemporary with Abbot Richard of Clairvaux's buildings at Fountains, though on a smaller scale. To the west of the cloister are the substantial remains of the guest hall, excavated in the 1980s. Most of the precinct, which is bisected by the A65, can be traced from its earthworks.

Roche Abbey

A grand-daughter of Fountains, Roche Abbey lies on the south side of the A634 between Maltby and Blyth in South Yorkshire. The site is managed by English Heritage and is open to the public from Easter to the end of October. There is a charge for admission.

At the entrance to the site are the substantial remains of the inner gatehouse, the best preserved example of a Cistercian inner gate in England, though all the buildings of the outer and inner courts have gone, buried below parterres laid by Capability Brown in the late eighteenth century. Brown similarly levelled and buried the greater part of the church and cloister ranges, though these have been excavated and displayed. The principal survivor is the east wall of the transepts and the short presbytery which survive to full height, preserved as an eye-catcher in Brown's landscape park. Their quality explains why the abbey was described as 'magnificent' by a fourteenth-century visitor. Near to the gate house and abbot's house are collections of architectural detail recovered by excavation.

Sawley Abbey

Another grand-daughter of Fountains, Sawley Abbey lies on the north side of the A59 to the north-east of Clitheroe in Lancashire (though the site was in Yorkshire until 1974). It is managed by the Heritage Trust for the North West on behalf of English Heritage, and is open daily throughout the year. There is no charge for admission.

The transepts and first bay of the nave survive to reasonable height, together with the lower walls of an extended presbytery. The cloister ranges can all be traced as low walling, excavated in the 1850s, 1930s and 1980s. Around the central buildings, a small precinct is defined by exceptionally good earthworks, all on private land, which can be seen either from public roads or from the cloister area. There is a small collection of detached architectural detail displayed on site.

Byland Abbey

Founded from Furness via Calder Abbey, Byland moved to its third and final site in 1177. The site lies to the south of the A170 between Helmsley and Thirsk in North Yorkshire, close to the village of Coxwold. The ruins are managed by English Heritage and are open from Easter to the end of October; there is a charge for admission.

Substantial remains of the church and cloister buildings are set within a large precinct (largely on private land) defined by good earthworks, many of which can be seen from the monument. A fragment of the inner gatehouse survives across the road to Oldstead to the west of the church. Byland has produced an exceptional collection of architectural detail, some of which has been re-erected on site, and more of which is displayed in a small museum on the south side of the monument.

Jervaulx Abbey

A daughter house of Byland, Jervaulx Abbey lies on the east side of the A6108 between Masham and Middleham in North Yorkshire. The site is privately owned but the ruins are open to the public at any reasonable time. There is a charge for admission.

The ruins at Jervaulx, first excavated in the early nineteenth century and incorporated in a garden, are a delight. Unlike any other site they have not been tidied up for display but left very much as they were found, with loose architectural detail piled up on the low walls close to where it was found, enabling lost buildings to be easily reconstructed. Although the church is heavily ruined, a great deal remains of the cloister ranges, infirmary, abbot's house, and meat kitchen.

152

THE ABBOTS OF FOUNTAINS

The story of Fountains Abbey is inevitably centred on the work and reputation of its abbots. A full list is known and is given below. The numbers they are given are the numbers they were accorded in the Middle Ages, and those who were not numbered were felt by the convent to have ruled unwisely or brought the monastery into disrepute. After their names, a brief résumé of their previous and later careers, if known, is given, followed by the dates of their abbacies:

1. *Richard I*, Prior of York Abbey — 1132-1139
2. *Richard II*, Sacrist of York Abbey — 1139-1143
3. *Henry Murdac*, Abbot of Vauclair, became Archbishop of York 1147, died 1153 — 1144-1147
   Maurice, sub-Prior of Durham, Abbot of Rievaulx, resigned and returned to Rievaulx — 1147-1148
   Thorold, monk of Rievaulx, resigned, became Abbot of Trois Fontaines — 1148-1150
4. *Richard of Clairvaux*, monk of Clairvaux, Abbot of Vauclair — 1150-1170
5. *Robert of Pipewell*, Abbot of Pipewell — 1170-1180
6. *William of Newminster*, Canon of Guisborough, Abbot of Newminster — 1180-1190
7. *Ralph Haget*, monk of Fountains, Abbot of Kirkstall — 1190-1203
8. *John of York*, Cellarer of Fountains, Abbot of Louth Park — 1203-1211
9. *John of Hessle*, became Bishop of Ely — 1211-1220
10. *John of Kent*, Cellarer of Fountains — 1220-1247
11. *Stephen of Eston*, Cellarer of Fountains, Abbot of Sawley, Abbot of Newminster — 1247-1252
12. *William of Allerton*, Prior of Fountains — 1253-1258
13. *Adam* — 1258-1259
14. *Alexander* — 1259-1265
15. *Reginald* — 1265-1274
    Peter Ayling, resigned 1279, died 1282 — 1274-1279
16. *Nicholas* — 1279
17. *Adam Ravensworth* — 1280-1284
    Henry Otley, probably resigned 1289, died 1290 — 1284-1289
    Robert Thornton, probably resigned 1290, died 1306 — 1289-1290

18. *Robert Bishopton* — 1290-1311
19. *William Rigton* — 1311-1316
20. *Walter Coxwold*, resigned 1336, died 1338 — 1316-1336
21. *Robert Copgrove* — 1336-1346
22. *Robert Monkton* — 1346-1369
23. *William Gower*, resigned 1384, died 1390 — 1369-1384
24. *Robert Burley* — 1384-1410
    Roger Frank, monk of Fountains, deposed 1413 — 1410-1413
25. *John Ripon*, Cellarer of Fountains, Abbot of Meaux — 1414-1435
26. *Thomas Paslew*, resigned 1442, died 1443 — 1435-1442
27. *John Martin* — 1442
28. *John Greenwell*, monk of Fountains, Abbot of Waverley, commissary of the Abbot of Cîteaux — 1442-1471
29. *Thomas Swinton*, Prior of Fountains, resigned 1478 — 1471-1478
30. *John Darnton*, Cellarer of Fountains, commissary of the abbot of Cîteaux — 1479-1495
31. *Marmaduke Huby*, monk, bursar, and Cellarer of Fountains, Master of St Mary Magdalene Hospital and Commissary of the Abbot of Cîteaux — 1495-1526
32. *William Thirsk*, Commissary of the Abbot of Cîteaux, resigned 1536, executed 1537 — 1526-1536
33. *Marmaduke Bradley*, monk of Fountains, prebendary Thorpe, Master of St Mary Magdalene Hospital, surrendered his abbey 1539, Died 1553 — 1536-1539

GLOSSARY

Antiphonary

A church service book which contains verses of the psalms and other traditional passages from the scriptures which were sung as responses (antiphons), often alternating between groups of choir monks.

Apse

The rounded termination of a chapel, aisle, or east end of a church or similar building, normally of eleventh- or twelfth-century date

Arcade

A series of arches carried on piers, as for instance between the main vessel of a church and an aisle, that carries the superstructure of the building.

Ashlar

Square-cut stone laid in regular courses to make the face of a wall.

Bay

The structural division of a building, normally emphasised in its architecture by vertical divisions, the placing of piers and buttresses.

Bercary

From the Latin *bercaria* a monastic sheep ranch, signifying not only buildings but also associated pastures and enclosures in open country.

Buttress

The localised widening of a wall at its bay divisions to provide additional support against the outward pressure exerted by roofs and vaults in a masonry building.

Bloomery

A furnace for smelting iron ore.

Capital

The decorative top of a pier or column which carries the springing of the arches of an arcade, often highly carved and painted, or similarly the decorated top of a wall shaft or nook-shaft on a door or window.

Carucate

A unit of land that could be tilled by one plough in a season, generally between 48.5 and 56.5ha.

Clerestorey

The upper storey of an aisled building, particularly a church, which was provided with windows to light the central vessel.

Corbel

A stone bracket, often carved, that projected from a wall-face to support either timber-work, a wall-shaft, or the springing of a vault.

Crossing

The point at which the principal axes of a cruciform church meet at the junction of nave, transepts, and presbytery. Normally, it was marked architecturally by a tower and was the preferred location of the monks' choir stalls.

Garth

An enclosed yard or paddock, normally associated with a particular building or group of buildings, for instance the bake house garth or common stable garth.

Interdict

The prohibition by the Pope or diocesan bishop of a person, institution, diocese, or country to celebrate divine service within churches or chapels.

Jamb

The side of a door or window frame.

Laver

A washing-place, normally placed in the cloister but sometimes also in the infirmary and other buildings, supplied with a piped water-supply, and often distinguished by its architectural sophistication.

Lay brother

A monastic servant subject to the same discipline as the choir monks but unlettered and responsible for the day-to-day servicing of the community. Lay brothers or *conversi* (literally 'converts') comprised the major element in early Cistercian monasteries where they were used to develop and farm substantial estates, but most orders actually had them in small numbers.

Mark

A currency of account rather than of coin which was valued at 13s 4d (£0.66).

Nave

The central vessel of an aisled building. In the monastic church it signifies the long or western arm of the church which might be partly used by the laity or by lay brothers.

Parclose

A wooden screen, often with elaborate decoration, that was used to divide a chapel from the main body of the church, or to divide chapels from each other.

Pentice

A passage or corridor running along the side of a building, its single-pitch (or pent) roof being carried on corbels in the wall of that building. Such corridors were normally of timber construction and have left little trace.

Pier

A free-standing masonry column that supports an arcade

Presbytery

The eastern arm of a monastic church that contained the enclosure of the high altar to the east of the monks' choir.

Pulpitum

The screen that closed the west end of the monks' choir, either of stone or timber.

Quarry

A cut piece of window glass or regular shape, often in the form of a square or diamond, that was fitted into a lead framework to make up a decorative pattern. The word comes from the Norman French *carré* which means 'squared'.

Respond

A half-pier placed against a wall at the end of an arcade.

Retable

A shelf of frame enclosing decorative panels above and behind an altar, often with a figure or symbols of the saint celebrated there.

Rood screen

The screen that closes off the nave from the monks' part of the church, normally set to the east of the nave altar, with doors through it to either side of the altar. There was normally a loft over it which carried images of the Virgin, St John, and the Christ crucified, which themselves constituted the 'rood'.

Simony

The buying or selling of any church office, and by extension, the buying or selling of church property.

String-course

A horizontal moulding used to level up the coursing of a rubble wall and to mark the structural divisions of elevations, for instance at the level of window sills or below a parapet.

Transept

The north and south arms of a cruciform church to either side of the crossing, and called the cross-aisle in medieval sources. They provided additional space for chapels.

Transom

The horizontal division of lights in a multi-light window.

Undercroft

A vaulted ground-floor or semi-subterranean room, of secondary importance to the room above and often only used for storage.

Vaccary

From the Latin *vaccaria*, a monastic cattle ranch, its buildings, paddocks, and pastures.

Vault

The fire-proof ceiling of a room. Vaults vary greatly in complexity, from simple barrel vaults to elaborate ceilings divided into panels by decorative and moulded ribs.

Wayleave

An agreement with a neighbouring landowner or his tenant to move stock and produce over his land. Such arrangements were common in the Middle Ages when the present network of public roads did not exist and land was often difficult to access.

INDEX